Elevate

16 Boarding Schools and the Practice of Holistic Education

Jake Weld
and
Jeremy McGeorge

Elevate

16 Boarding Schools and the Practice of Holistic Education

Jake Weld
and
Jeremy McGeorge

Elevate: 16 Boarding Schools and the Practice of Holistic Education

By Jake Weld and Jeremy McGeorge

© 2026 Considered Practice, LLC. All rights reserved.
Individual chapters are copyrighted by their respective authors.

Cover design and layout by Jake Weld.

No part of this book may be reproduced or transmitted in any form or by any means, electronic or mechanical, including photocopying, recording, or by any information storage and retrieval system, without prior written permission of the publisher, except in the case of brief quotations embodied in critical articles, reviews, or other uses permitted by copyright law.

The authors of Chapters 3–18 retain copyright in their individual contributions and have granted Considered Practice, LLC a nonexclusive license to publish their work as part of this volume.

This book is set in Garamond. For typographic consistency, mid-sentence pauses in body text are set with en dashes (–); em dashes are not used.

First Edition, 2026
ISBN 979-8-9949642-0-0

For permission requests visit www.elevateschools.org

An imprint of Considered Practice, LLC
www.consideredpractice.org
South Burlington, Vermont

Dedication

This book is dedicated to the faculty and staff of holistic educational communities – those whose daily, often unseen labor makes community real.

Without them, these communities would not be possible.

Table Of Contents

Preface

This book began with a simple aim: to capture and share the stories of a small group of boarding schools that, in our experience, are doing something thoughtful, and often quiet, in how they approach holistic education. These ecosystems are inhabited not only by ideals, but by people – the adults who enact them, the adolescents who live within them, and the families who choose to engage with residential learning communities during a formative and consequential period of a young person's life. Along the way, we learned that telling those stories honestly required as much restraint as enthusiasm, and as much clarity about what this book is not as what it is.

The idea for *Elevate* took shape over dinner in Newport, Rhode Island. We were in town for a professional conference focused on education and mental health, and after a long day of sessions and conversations, we found ourselves doing what friends often do when the formal agenda ends – trading stories. We talked about schools we knew well, students we had worked with, places that felt alive in ways that were difficult to quantify but simple to recognize, and we considered what elements fueled this distinction. It became clear to us that something meaningful, but often quiet, is happening on a number of boarding school campuses, and that those stories are worth slowing down to notice.

We were also aware, from the start, of the baggage that comes with any conversation about private boarding schools in the United States. These institutions sit inside a complicated history shaped by privilege, exclusion, aspiration, innovation, and contradiction. That history matters. It shapes who these schools serve, how they are perceived, and the responsibilities they carry. We were not interested in writing a book that ignored those realities or one that pretended to resolve them neatly. Instead, we wanted to acknowledge the tensions honestly and then look closely at how contemporary schools are navigating them in practice.

Early in the project, we faced a choice. We could write *about* specific schools by interpreting, evaluating, and filtering their unique work through our own voices, or we could invite schools to speak for themselves, directly and in their own language, about the communities they are actively trying to create – and we could then write about what we learned when taking a holistic view of that landscape. We chose the latter. That decision came with tradeoffs. It meant accepting variation in articulation, resisting the urge to polish or correct, and allowing schools to reveal not only what they do well, but how they understand themselves at this particular moment in time. We believe that how institutions tell their own stories – what they emphasize, what they gloss over, and what they assume goes without saying is, itself, meaningful. This book is built on that belief.

Our own perspectives inevitably shape this work. We both spent formative years working in boarding schools in the early 2000s, just as technology, social media, and shifting cultural expectations were beginning to collide with adolescence in new ways. Since then, our careers have kept us closely connected to education and mental health, giving us a front-row seat to the ways schools have adapted – sometimes awkwardly, sometimes creatively – to rising anxiety, changing family dynamics, and a world where access to information has far outpaced opportunities for meaning, responsibility, and belonging.

Great boarding schools today are no longer judged solely by where their graduates go next, or by how rigorously they deliver academic content. They are increasingly asked to do something harder: to create environments that support intellectual growth while also fostering emotional resilience, social awareness, agency, and purpose. The schools included here represent a range of responses to that challenge. They differ in size, mission, and population, but each is grappling, intentionally, with what it means to educate the whole person in a complex and rapidly changing world.

This book does not argue that these schools have solved the challenges of education, or that their models should be universally replicated. It does not claim to measure outcomes or prove effectiveness. What it offers instead is a snapshot: a collection of self-described community portraits that, taken together, illuminate patterns, tensions, and possibilities in holistic education. Its contribution is in framing a space in which to listen, and then following that attention with synthesis. Our hope is that these stories serve as points of reflection – for parents considering educational environments, for educators designing programs and cultures, and for anyone curious about how young people grow when communities are built with care and intention.

We offer *Elevate* not as a verdict, but as an invitation – to look closely, to think critically, and to consider what becomes possible when education is intentionally approached as a lived experience of meaning and connection in the present, rather than solely as preparation for the future.

– Jake Weld & Jeremy McGeorge

Chapter 1

Introduction

Secondary education carries an outsized burden. These are the years when young people are asked, sometimes directly, often implicitly, to begin answering questions about who they are, what they care about, and how they will participate in the world beyond school. At the same time, the institutions charged with supporting that development are increasingly evaluated through a narrow set of outcomes: grades, standardized tests, college placement, and rankings that attempt to compress complex human growth into clean comparisons.

We are not indifferent to those measures. They matter. But over years of working in and around schools, and through ongoing conversations with educators, clinicians, school leaders, and families, we have become increasingly convinced that they are insufficient for describing what actually helps adolescents grow into capable, grounded, and engaged adults. Again and again, the environments that most held our attention were not those chasing innovation for its own sake or optimizing for external validation, but those quietly designing communities where responsibility, belonging, and purpose were built into daily life. This book emerges from that shared appreciation, admiration, and curiosity.

Why Boarding Schools?

Boarding schools are not inherently better than other educational models, nor are they appropriate for all students or families. They are, however, unusually legible systems. When students live, learn, eat, work, and spend their unstructured time within the same community, the relationship between values, structure, and experience becomes harder to obscure. What a school believes about adolescents – how much they are trusted, how responsibility is conferred, how mistakes are handled – shows up not only in classrooms, but in dormitories, dining halls, work programs, and the rhythms of daily life.

For our purposes, boarding schools function less as the universal ideal and more as lenses through which to examine how educational communities are intentionally constructed. The integration of residential and academic life makes visible assumptions that often remain implicit elsewhere. In that sense, these schools offer a useful window into questions that extend far beyond their campuses.

Adolescence as a Developmental Window

Adolescence is not simply a bridge between childhood and adulthood; it is a formative period in its own right. It is a time of identity formation, increasing cognitive complexity, emotional volatility, and a growing desire for autonomy and belonging. It is also a period during which young people are acutely sensitive to whether they are trusted, needed, and taken seriously. Educational institutions hold disproportionate influence during this period, and the choices schools make about structure, authority, and responsibility carry ethical weight beyond academic preparation alone. In boarding environments, where much of an adolescent's daily experience unfolds within a residential community, that responsibility is intensified rather than diluted.

Many educational systems respond to this developmental reality by increasing support while quietly reducing responsibility. Structure becomes protection; oversight becomes control. In some contexts, this is necessary.

In others, it inadvertently communicates low expectations about students' capacity to contribute meaningfully to their communities.

The schools featured in this book approach adolescence differently. In varied ways, they treat young people not as problems to be managed, but as participants in a shared endeavor. Responsibility is not postponed until graduation; it is practiced daily. Independence is not assumed; it is scaffolded. Belonging is not incidental; it is intentionally cultivated. These approaches are not without risk or tension, but they reflect a common belief: adolescents grow best when they are trusted with real roles in real communities.

How to Read This Book

The chapters that follow are written by the schools themselves. Each school was invited to tell its own story and to reflect on the practices, structures, and commitments that shape its approach to holistic education without a prescribed framework beyond basic context, length, and introductory demographic information. This choice reflects a central premise of this project: that how institutions understand their own work – and how they choose to describe it – what they emphasize, what they assume, what they highlight, and what they leave unsaid, is itself meaningful.

As a result, the chapters vary in tone and emphasis. Some are reflective and narrative; others are more programmatic or declarative. We resisted the urge to standardize these contributions, believing that variation is not a flaw to be corrected but a value worth noticing. Taken together, these differences offer insight into how schools translate values into daily practice under very different conditions, for different students, and within distinct institutional contexts. What emerges from this approach is clear differentiation among the individual schools, alongside a recognizable convergence around how holistic educational communities are imagined and enacted.

This book is not a ranking, an evaluation, or a comparative study. It does not attempt to validate outcomes or offer prescriptions. Instead, it presents a snapshot in time: a collection of self-described community portraits, assembled to be read attentively and critically, with an eye toward patterns that emerge through accumulation rather than direction or argument.

What follows should be read neither as endorsement nor as proof, but as an invitation – to look closely at how intentional educational communities are built, to consider what adolescents may need beyond academic preparation alone, and to reflect on how daily structures, expectations, and relationships shape young people over time.

The schools included here were selected through an intentionally unscientific, advisory-informed process shaped by experience, dialogue, and repeated encounters with institutions grappling seriously with similar questions. A fuller account of that process, along with the perspectives and influences that informed it, appears in **Appendix A**.

Chapter 2

Context, Tradition, and Tension

Boarding schools in the United States occupy a complicated and often uneasy position in the educational landscape. They are frequently associated with privilege, exclusivity, and tradition – and in many cases, those associations are grounded in real history. At the same time, boarding schools have long functioned as sites of experimentation: places where ideas about curriculum, community life, governance, and adolescent development have been tested with a degree of autonomy not always available in public systems.

Any serious examination of boarding schools must hold both realities at once. To do otherwise, either by romanticizing or dismissing them, obscures more than it reveals.

Historical Roots and Divergent Purposes

The earliest American boarding schools emerged in the colonial period, often connected to religious communities, classical academies, or regional efforts to educate young people for leadership, ministry, or civic life. Some were explicitly designed to serve elite populations; others were founded with reformist intentions, offering alternatives to the prevailing educational norms of their time. Over the centuries, these strands intertwined, producing institutions that often combined innovation and conservatism in complex and sometimes contradictory ways.

By the late nineteenth and early twentieth centuries, boarding schools had become more formally established as residential academic institutions, particularly in the Northeast and Mid-Atlantic regions. This period coincided with broader cultural and educational debates about childhood, adolescence, authority, and citizenship. Questions about how young people learn best, how much autonomy they should be granted, and what role schools should play in moral and social development were actively contested – and boarding schools, by virtue of their residential structure, became visible arenas for exploring those questions in practice.

Any discussion of boarding schools in North America also exists alongside a fundamentally different and deeply harmful history: the system of Indian Boarding Schools created to forcibly separate Indigenous children from their families, cultures, and languages. The schools examined in this book are not part of that system, nor do they share its purpose or design. This history is named here not to draw equivalence, but to clarify context: boarding schools have never been morally neutral institutions, and the authority they hold over young people carries ethical weight. Any contemporary examination of residential education must be read with that reality in view.

Progressivism, Experience, and Its Discontents

Progressive education gained prominence during the late nineteenth and early twentieth centuries, shaped by thinkers who challenged the assumption that schooling should prioritize rote instruction, compliance, and standardized outcomes. John Dewey and others argued that education should be rooted in experience, community participation, and the development of judgment rather than mere information transfer. Learning, in this view, was inseparable from lived context.

Yet progressive education has always carried internal tensions. Even Dewey later expressed concern that some schools invoking progressive ideals confused freedom with the absence of structure, mistaking loosened authority for meaningful agency. His critique was not of experience-based learning itself, but of its shallow or indulgent application – where rebellion against authority replaced responsibility, and structure was dismantled rather than reimagined. That critique remains relevant today.

Structure, Freedom, and the Adolescent Question

The tension between freedom and structure runs through nearly every educational reform movement. On one end lies rigid control, where compliance is mistaken for learning. On the other lies unbounded choice, where the absence of expectation undermines growth. Boarding schools – because they integrate academic, residential, and social life – make this tension particularly visible.

Adolescence complicates this further. It is a developmental period marked by increasing cognitive complexity, heightened sensitivity to belonging and fairness, and a growing desire for autonomy alongside a continued need for guidance. Schools that treat adolescents either as children to be managed or as adults to be left alone often miss the developmental middle ground.

The schools featured in this book approach that middle ground in different ways. While their structures vary, many share an emphasis on pairing freedom with responsibility, autonomy with expectation, and independence with accountability. These ideas are neither new nor uniformly applied, but they are difficult to sustain in practice – especially within institutions shaped by tradition, parental expectation, and external accountability.

Privilege, Access, and Structural Reality

Any discussion of boarding schools must also grapple honestly with questions of access and privilege. Tuition-based education exists within broader social and economic systems that advantage some families over others. While many boarding schools have expanded financial aid, outreach, and mission-driven enrollment practices, none operate outside the realities of inequality.

This book does not attempt to resolve those tensions, nor does it present boarding schools as universal solutions. Instead, it treats them as situated communities – working within historical, financial, and cultural constraints – designing and implementing environments they believe support adolescent growth. Naming those constraints is not an indictment; it is a prerequisite for reading the chapters that follow with clarity rather than illusion.

Boarding Schools as a Lens

Today, boarding schools educate only a small fraction of secondary-school students in the United States. Their scale alone precludes them from serving as models for broad systemic reform. Their relevance in this context lies elsewhere.

Because academic, residential, social, and extracurricular life are integrated within a single institutional framework, boarding schools offer unusually clear insight into how educational values are operationalized. Decisions about trust, discipline, independence, community norms, and adult authority are not abstract; they shape students' lived experience every day. In this sense, boarding schools function less as exemplars to be replicated and more as lenses through which to examine how educational environments are intentionally constructed.

Reading Forward

Without historical and sociological grounding, conversations about holistic education risk becoming either romantic or dismissive. Accounts of autonomy can sound indulgent without context; accounts of structure can sound authoritarian. Read together, they point to something more complicated: institutions wrestling – often imperfectly – with enduring questions about adolescence, authority, belonging, and responsibility.

The schools included in this book do not speak with one voice, nor do they arrive at shared conclusions. Their differences reflect a central reality of holistic education: it is not a formula, but a practice shaped by values, people, place, and time. The purpose of this chapter has not been to resolve debates about boarding schools or progressive education, but to offer enough context to read what follows with attentiveness and discernment. The deeper patterns, and the harder questions, emerge later – once these schools have had the opportunity to speak for themselves.

In the chapters that follow, we turn our attention to a collection of intentionally designed educational communities. Each chapter offers a self-described portrait of how a particular school understands its mission, structures daily life, and supports adolescent development within its own context.

These schools are not presented as universal models or solutions to broader educational challenges. They are offered instead as situated examples – distinct, imperfect, and thoughtful – of how values are translated into lived practice. What they share is not sameness, but seriousness: a sustained effort to align purpose with process in the daily work of educating young people.

The Putney School

Location: Putney, Vermont

Year Founded: 1935

Grades Served: 9–12 + Post Grad

Total Enrollment: 225

Percent Boarding: 72%

Percent Non-White: 28%

Percent From Out of State: 34%

Percent From Out of Country: 13%

2025–26 School Year Tuition: $83,000

Percent Who Receive Financial Aid: 40%

School Website: www.putneyschool.org

Head of School: Danny O'Brien

The Putney School

Chapter Completed By

Kate Knopp, Assistant Head of School
& Danny O'Brien, Head of School

When the administrator-on-duty phone rings at 10:00 on a Saturday evening, my heart skips a beat. It is not usually a good sign. The voice on the other end of the call surprised me; the tenth-grade student's voice was full of energy. Dom had a problem, alright, but not one I expected. He had stopped by The Putney School's barn on his way back to his dorm room to check on our sixty-head dairy herd. One of the cows had just given birth; Dom could not find our farm manager, who seemed always available, so he called the AOD phone number.

Dom asked, "What do I do? I'm not sure what to do?" I paused. This was not something I had learned at head-of-school training camp. Would Google have an answer? I reached for my computer and typed in the search bar. As I did, Dom began telling me what he had already done. The words on my screen matched his words in my ear. Make sure the mother pays attention to the newborn calf. Ensure the mom and calf are warm. Give them hay and water. Alone in our school's barn on a Saturday night, without the aid of the technology I had in my hand, Dom had done all the right things.

The cow did her work that night, and Dom did his. He used the knowledge he had gained from working with the cows and applied that knowledge, then he checked in to see if what he'd done was working. For the rest of his life, Dom will have that story to tell. As it evolves, Dom's role at the barn will undoubtedly grow; his confidence in himself to figure out the best way to tend to the cows will grow. The details matter very little.

What matters more is the sense of purpose Dom found that evening; he felt needed and stepped into responsibility for the animals. An adolescent entered a situation where he was needed; he stepped up and made himself useful.

That sense of being needed; the satisfaction that comes from doing something important, well... this motivates all of us. As Tim Klein and Belle Liang write in their book *How to Navigate Life*, "(Students who are engaged) have a better sense of their own identity, take more initiative, and are more self-directive." Dom may not work on a farm again in his life after Putney. His experiences on the farm, though, teach skills that will transfer to other parts of his life. What he learned that night is that he can rely on himself to solve problems. He can act with limited knowledge; he can assess his own work and seek resources, in this case, an adult with Google – to be sure that what he'd done was right.

Putney was founded in 1935 by Carmelita Hinton, an acolyte of John Dewey. Carmelita Hinton was a woman of grand ambition; helping adolescents find purpose was only a part of her dream for The Putney School.

She wanted much more. In 1935, she saw a darkening world. Her generation was not doing the job: fascism, racism, inequality, and rank individualism were ascendant. Hinton believed the world could do better, and she believed teenagers were the ones who could rise to the needs of the time. We might just be in a similar moment in time.

Armed with a vision for a better world and an unerring belief in the capacity of teenagers, Carmelita purchased a hilltop farm in Vermont with views as expansive as her dreams. What school should be was already obvious to her. The challenge was to connect her ideas, like pieces of a complex puzzle, to the idea of what a school could be.

What could teenagers do? What did they need to experience to develop the skills and dispositions needed to uplift the world?

- First, extraordinary academic preparation. Hinton proclaimed that Putney students would work harder and learn more because they would generate and refine their own ideas rather than regurgitate the lectures of teachers. Carmelita was uncompromising on one point: The Putney School would compete against elite New England schools for top academic talent, and prepare students for success in college and career like no other school did.
- Second, a prominent place for creativity and innovation. Hinton saw appreciation of the arts as central to a "good life," and she designed a program where students would grant the arts great prestige, experimenting, creating, inspiring, and being inspired. Arts, the doing of them unleashes engagement and activism in community; teenagers who practice sharing their creativity engage in the world more easily.
- Third, a chance to feel ownership. Hinton believed that ownership propelled achievement. Students who have real responsibility practice using their authority. Students would milk dairy cows, clean their dorms, wash dishes in the dining hall, and, in the early days, even build their own dorms and classrooms. They would also contribute to decisions about curriculum and governance, going as far as serving as voting members of the board of trustees. In short, students would

learn to care deeply about the community, motivating them to work harder than they would otherwise to sustain and improve it.

- Fourth, care for both the natural and wider worlds. Hinton wanted her students to be hearty and healthy. Exposure to fresh air and physical exertion were part of the Putney experience from the beginning: climbing to the bald summit of nearby Mount Monadnock and learning to cross-country ski were as central to the Putney experience as the farm and classrooms. Hinton also made sure to cancel school so students and faculty could attend Vermont's famous town meetings.

Almost a century later, these pillars, student-driven academics, arts, work, and physical exertion, remain core to the Putney experience. They have stayed constant as our school has evolved. Putney has been known for many things through the years, but these core values remain.

Out of our commitment to the arts came leadership in music. For many years, we were an epicenter for classical music in the United States. Short of a conservatory, there was no school where classical music mattered more. Under legendary music director Norwood Hinckle, students flocked to Putney for the opportunity to learn and be part of such a culture. When studying and making music together, students rely on one another. They prepare, deepen their skills, and then show up to play so that the orchestra or band, or vocal ensemble can depend on them to do their part well. It is collaborative and experiential and builds community all at the same time. Every Thursday morning, we gather as a school for Sing; that 45-minute ritual is an animation of a Putney ethos of learning and playing together.

Putney's belief in immersion with the natural world and an active lifestyle meant leadership in Nordic skiing in the United States. Including

Bill Koch '72, the first American to medal in cross-country skiing in the Olympics, a half dozen Olympians have graduated from Putney School. Johnny Caldwell, the father of Nordic skiing in the United States, coached most of them during his fifty-year association with the school.

Our farm program attracts the admiration of agriculturists and farm educators everywhere. The 2023 World Cheese Awards – the most important cheese competition that exists – received over 4,500 entrants. Only seven "Super Gold" awards were given to U.S. cheesemakers, and two Super Golds were awarded to Parish Hill Creamery in Westminster, Vt. Parish Hill's milk comes from Putney School cows. Putney students milk and manage our herd every single day. Which is another way of saying that the milk that produces the best cheese in the United States is brought to market by a crew of teenagers. Look what teenagers can do!

Our students recently traveled to the Forging Foundation Forge Fair in Cleveland to participate in a blacksmithing competition. They competed against college students from across the country. And Putney students won the honor of best performance. They didn't set out to win, though; they were excited for the chance to bend metal with other artists and craftsmen. Their passion and drive to learn and "to do" landed them at a blacksmithing competition. "There were colleges at the competition that are producing mechanical engineers and have the equipment to analyze steel hardness and industrial machinery to help them press and create tools. Our little high school won the best performance," recalled sculpture teacher Brian Quarrier '05.

You can find achievements like these on any corner of Putney's campus. Other schools have success stories like these, too. What sets Putney apart, however, is what propels our students.

Where is the drive for excellence and innovation coming from?

At Putney, it's about igniting the interest and engagement that lives within the students. The campus culture invites them to explore their interests. They test them out in the barn, the playing fields, the woods and fields of southern Vermont, and our arts studios. (Where else can you find a forge, ceramics, jewelry, painting and sculpture, and dance in one place?) The faculty create spaces for students to explore and soar. What questions do you have? What topics do you want to know more about? Faculty help students hone skills and acquire knowledge about topics that inspire them–this is core to the Putney model.

High school is a good time to experiment with your interests and explore your talents. Teenagers should try out many interests before they stake a claim and start to solidify an identity. Because our campus is filled with scientists, farmers, artists, and more, and our curriculum is designed to be flexible and student-driven, students can pick up a camera or take a jewelry-making class or throw a pot and be inspired for the first time by doing something new to them. Sometimes they discover a passion they could not have predicted.

Liam, for instance, thinks of himself as a writer and a student of history. He is a serious reader. He signed up for a Photography class as part of the Evening Arts program; twice a week, students explore art classes in the evening hours. Liam fell in love with an analog camera and the processes of developing and printing photographs. He designed an independent study the next year and leaned in to develop skills he hadn't set out to discover. Liam has received multiple awards for his work, including a Scholastic National Gold Medal for his portrait, "Glowing," as well as being named the 2025 Ilford High School Photographer of the Year.

How we teach and how we think about learning is a distinctive feature of Putney. When we say that we are "student-centered," we mean that students design their own learning, literally. Twice a year, we give students ten days of academic time – to do. They write proposals. That process teaches them how to take a nascent idea and develop a plan to pursue it. They might build a telescope, or a small boat, or repurpose a propane tank into a smoker for barbecuing, write a play or a song, weave a wall hanging, or start a pollinator garden on campus. Students generate an idea. Faculty advisors and project week sponsors offer critique and support as students plan.

After two or three years at Putney, this process becomes familiar; students gain self-awareness about how they learn, how they manage their time, and how best to use resources to meet their goals. Project Weeks culminate in a celebration of sharing. Student work is showcased in a gallery exhibition, and some present their work in a TED Talk style. They share not only what they did with their Project Week but also what they learned about how they handle failures and how they recovered from them. Talking about how they learn is a regular and celebrated part of our conversation about growth and excellence at Putney.

Educators use many vehicles to motivate students. Some, like giving direct instruction or reinforcing metrics for success, create short bursts of momentum. These tactics, like adding paper to a fire, can get students over a finish line, but they burn out quickly. More challenging approaches, such as asking questions to find out what students love, helping them find passions, and giving them space to explore what is important to them, these approaches are like adding large logs to a flame. The burn is slow – sometimes harder to catch – but lasting. The Putney School favors the latter approach almost every time.

Faculty at Putney are steeped in content knowledge, and they are students of learning; they are as interested in how learning happens for each student as they are in their area of expertise. Our faculty step back so that students have to step up. Picture a toddler discovering their legs are meant for walking. Parents back away to create some space, to offer the infant an open space, a challenge. Adults cheer and clap and encourage the child to put one foot in front of the other. The thrill of accomplishment and the confidence that rushes in after the success live with the newly mobile child. The same rush comes to Putney students when they've set their own goals and stretched themselves in the process of achieving them. Think about Dom realizing he had done all the right things to support the cow and her newborn calf that night. He hung up the phone feeling confident he had used his knowledge well – on his own, and with the support of an adult to confirm his actions.

Our students find their purpose in every corner of our campus. This is a lot to pack into a small school on a Vermont hillside! We believe in boarding school because of all we are trying to achieve in a single day, year, or four. Students' "aha" moment can happen at 9:00 am on a Monday or in the barn at 10:00 on a Saturday evening. This requires enormous time and effort – to build a community that needs teenagers to engage and to take responsibility for it. The results, though, can be astounding. Our alumni matriculate to the finest colleges and universities, finding success in those places because they want to learn and not because they have to. They become artists, politicians, and tech leaders because they see what they have to offer the world, not because it is expected of them.

Putney believes in students. We trust they can do hard things; we keep pushing when they fall short of their potential. We remind them that their education is their own. At the same time, there is no "Putney recipe" for how to get there. Putney knows students will do better when they mix the ingredients for their challenges and growth on their own; ask their own questions, and design their own learning. We trust them to make good use of the freedom to choose their academic and experiential learning challenges.

Putney adults convince students they can do hard things; we help them to know they can do more than they think they can. Faculty refocus students when they wander or languish. And adults and students alike seek all sorts of ways to promote ingenuity, collaboration, and passion for learning in our community.

That this is how students achieve their potential is well documented. "In 35 randomized control trials in 18 countries, researchers found that when students are allowed some opportunity to take their own initiative, they are more engaged in class and better able to master new skills, they have better grades and fewer problems with peers – and they are happier, too," wrote Jenny Anderson and Rebecca Winthrop in the New York Times. It's not a new idea. Putney has been believing in students' capacity to be responsible and capable citizens since 1935. They don't always get it right, but they have an authentic learning community in which to make mistakes and learn.

Putney's secret sauce is to balance accountability and agency. Agency without accountability reduces learning opportunities; it is often chaotic. Students learn in isolation and forget their responsibility to things greater than themselves. Similarly, accountability without agency promotes shallow learning and a culture of compliance. It is, at best, boring. Overemphasis on accountability values standardized test scores, class rank, and college placement. There is little lasting, joyful, or motivating in it. We aim to strike a balance.

What the world is figuring out today, Carmelita Hinton understood in 1935 when she founded the Putney School. The Putney experiment continues; we continue to think deeply and critically about how best to invite adolescents to engage and learn, and solve real problems. The world in 2025 is flooded with easy access to information, and new technologies have changed education considerably since the advent of personal computers and the internet, but teenagers still need to learn who they are and how they want to participate in their lives and communities. Now more than ever, they need to discover their grit and independence; the curriculum at Putney, in and out of the classroom, is designed for them to practice those two essential skills. Achieving the fine balance between agency and accountability is as difficult as finding a clear radio signal in a rural part of an open road. You need to jiggle the dial, constantly. The balance is different for every student.

Add to grit and independence a sense of community and responsibility for a greater good. At Putney, we begin with respect for the capacity of young people, and we invite them to grow by engaging in the school community. We invite them to care for the animals, make art, build community, grow their capacity, ask questions, and test their ideas. We expect them to stretch and to fail, and we insist that they reflect on who they are as learners. Our students learn by doing; our faculty facilitates a process of proposing projects and setting goals, reflecting on and assessing the learning that the experience – a project week, an independent study, an exhibition – offers at the end. We believe in experience and our teachers are poised to support students who have an idea about designing and building an experience.

Putney is committed to this journey with every child in our care. Success in our classrooms, ski trails, and arts studios comes because our students care about what they do, and they see great purpose in it.

Dublin School

Location: Dublin, New Hampshire

Year Founded: 1935

Grades Served: 9–12

Total Enrollment: 165

Percent Boarding: 70%

Percent Non-White: 23%

Percent From Out of State: 65%

Percent From Out of Country: 13%

2025–26 School Year Tuition: $79,850

Percent Who Receive Financial Aid: 35%

School Website: www.dublinschool.org

Head of School: Brad Bates, Head of School (through June, 2026)
Sam Bicknell, Incoming Head of School

Dublin School

Chapter Completed By

Brad Bates, Head of School

From Students:

This is a place where it is more than possible, encouraged, to try new things, take risks, learn to grow, and become an empathetic member of society. I have found a community with people who are both similar and different, where I can be challenged in my thinking while also encouraged to keep asking questions (one of my favorite hobbies). The faculty are there for you in every aspect of life and are knowledgeable beyond their subject matter. Students are a part of school decisions, big and small, and truly shape the school from culture to class schedule.

There is always so much going on, from clubs to activities or just hanging out; every time you want to go do something, there is always someone who will join you.

From Parents:

There is so much to love about this school. The campus is absolutely gorgeous, the academics are challenging without being a grind, the teachers are dedicated, and the student body is amazingly diverse for rural NH. Due to the small size, there is space for everyone in any activity, and trying new things is actively encouraged.

The school changed my son's life. Previously, he was at a school that did not support kids who didn't fit the typical mold. He tried to be invisible and not stand out. He was unhappy. Dublin's welcoming community helped him gradually open up: he is coming into his own and expressing his true self. In a year, he made a turnaround, both academically and in sports. He is thriving at Dublin.

Dublin School was founded in 1935 in the spirit of being an educational adventure, and it remains true to its roots almost one hundred years later. Paul Lehmann, the school's founder, wrote in the introduction to his history of the school that, "as we embarked upon the adventure, other characteristics within ourselves came to the surface. First, there was to be independence – freedom, if you will – to work within the framework of our own abilities and our own consciences. We were not to be restrained; our efforts were not to be colored by outside influences contrary to our beliefs. This did not mean we did not listen, or observe, or read. Indeed, we did. But we adopted only what we believed to be sound in pursuing our goal." And that goal involved a unique and timeless approach to educating young people to see beyond the limits of who they think they can become.

Paul Lehmann chose the current campus location to ensure it was separated from the distractions of city life, situated in an area with strong cultural roots, and in a beautiful setting with commanding views of the surrounding land. He wanted to establish one of the strongest academic programs in New England, featuring highly experienced educators and a focus on the outdoors. He believed in combining academic learning with practical responsibility. Students continue to participate in "work gangs" to take care of the campus and serve the local community. He believed that Dublin alumni should be valuable members of society, living rich and meaningful lives.

Dublin School remains closely connected to its roots, believing that all schools were created for a specific reason. While Dublin School has undergone a significant renovation of its campus over the last fifteen years, much of the growth has been focused on returning to its core mission of developing curiosity, self-discipline, service, and a sense of community among its students. The school's motto, "Truth and Courage," is woven into the fabric of community discussions, expectations, and activities. Hiring, developing, and retaining an outstanding faculty who meet students where they are remains the school administration's laser focus. Faculty live on campus and teach, coach, and advise their students.

Dublin strives to be an intentionally small, academically focused institution that surprises its students with an unexpected array of opportunities for them to pursue. The school's size is intended to be large enough to operate a significant number of programs while remaining small enough for everyone in the community to know each other's names by the end of the first semester. With its large teaching staff, Dublin offers close to one hundred academic classes every year. Classrooms are designed around the Harkness style of learning with oval-shaped tables supporting intense discussions. Much of the education takes place with students sharing and refining their thoughts with students and teachers from a diverse range of backgrounds. In the spirit of the liberal arts, the curriculum inspires students to think across the boundaries of their independent subjects to build new understandings of the world around them. Dublin teachers adopt a mentor mindset with their students, setting high expectations while providing substantial support. While expectations are kept high, the adults work together to make sure that the program allows students the time and space to be curious learners.

Dublin is well known for its Learning Skills Program (LSP), which offers one-to-one support with highly trained learning specialists. With sessions built directly into students' schedules and learning specialists dynamically collaborating with other departments, classroom teachers, students' advisors, and one another, the program is deeply embedded into the very fabric of Dublin School. Students in LSP learn "how to learn" through intentional skills instruction in the context of their current coursework, while navigating the various strengths and challenges that characterize their personal academic experience. The program has been highly successful in helping its students access a rigorous college preparatory curriculum.

Dublin has a three-year arts, technology, and design academic requirement that forefronts the importance of creativity, expression, and identity in young people's lives. The visual arts program is highlighted by its groundbreaking art portfolio program. Advanced art students spend their afternoons in the fall and winter in either an art or music portfolio and are provided with individual studios to work on their projects. The studios are designed to be visible to younger artists so they can be inspired by art students who plan to study art in college. The strength of the program is evidenced by the disproportionate number of Scholastic Art Awards students have won over the last fifteen years. Woodworking has also emerged as a signature program with advanced classes building tiny houses, warming huts, and a lakeside sauna. Students can take ceramics, dance, music, photography, and combined art and technology classes. The recording studio stands as one of the most popular spaces on campus.

The school's Perkin Observatory takes advantage of the area's dark skies to provide an essential educational portal to the stars for the students. Regular programming invites students to the observatory for special viewings of astronomical events. Advanced astronomy students take astrophotography courses using the fully programmable cameras to track and shoot stars, nebulae, and galaxies for research purposes.

Senior Project offers students the opportunity to engage in a year-long, rigorous study centered around a question or topic that is of special interest to them. The course includes both a scholarly and a creative, or applied, component. Students are expected to meet college-level standards in independence, time management, and advanced analytical and creative problem-solving. Every student writes a research paper exploring the field or fields at the intersection of their project, documents their process with regular unit plans and reflections, works both with their Senior Project teacher and on- or off-campus mentors, and (when applicable) applies for funding for special workshops, internships, lessons, or materials necessary for the enhancement of their learning. Ultimately, each student channels their knowledge, skills, and passion into creating an original work that is shared with the community on Mayfair Weekend. The value of a capstone course like Senior Project is evident not only in the end products the students create but also in the journeys they undertake in the process.

Dublin's E.E. Ford Foundation Spanish Language Program focuses the whole school on learning one language while exploring many cultures. The goal is to teach students the art and science of language acquisition and appreciation through the study of Spanish, equipping them with the skills to learn other languages throughout their lifetime. The school travel program sends one trip to Patagonia and one trip to another Spanish-speaking country each year. Students participate in homestays and welcome foreign students to their homes and dormitory rooms during the school year. Students and faculty invite foreign speakers to campus for presentations and eat meals together, speaking in Spanish. The school has a "Patagonia Cafe" where students can eat snacks, practice their Spanish, drink coffee, and watch Spanish-language television.

Students and faculty on the school's Academic Committee developed a highly popular J-Term, collaborating to create two-week-long courses on a single subject, which are taught each January. Building off the mission to inspire curiosity, these ungraded classes allow students to delve deeply into a subject and learn for the sake of learning. Recent courses have included Crime Scene Investigation Dublin, the Supreme, Fiber Arts Extravaganza, Raku Pottery, Storytelling and Public Speaking, and Winter Wilderness Survival.

The Dublin School administration is obsessed with school culture. To them, it is the most crucial topic for discussion. One can have a wonderful campus, an outstanding faculty, and a strong program, but culture is the key to unlocking the power of people, place, and program. Every spring for the last ten years, the head of school and other faculty have taken the junior class to northern Maine for a whitewater rafting trip. The main goal of the journey is to return to campus with a statement of the kind of culture they want to create on campus when they return in the fall as seniors. They often focus on goals like school spirit, kindness, celebrating being young, and trying new things. Graduating seniors often speak to a culture that encouraged them to keep growing, challenge themselves, and seize opportunities by trying things they hadn't done before. The adults support school culture by seeking student voice in decision-making.

Student leadership opportunities have exploded in recent years. Student "proctors" help run the dormitories and lead the day students, Advancement and Enrollment Office interns gain valuable experience in the functioning of the school, weight room and kitchen supervisors learn essential management skills, student elected judicial board and academic committee members make sure student perspective is valued, student government works closely with the Dean of Students' office, and students on the head of school design committee meet with the school's architects and help design student-friendly spaces. Dublin finds that increasing student voice and leadership fosters belonging and helps students feel ownership of their education and their community.

Dublin School started as a typical northern New England school in a village. What began with one cedar-shingled cottage on a couple of acres has expanded to include multiple buildings, five hundred acres of land, and three boathouses on two different lakes. The town of Dublin, New Hampshire, just seventy-five miles from Boston, was widely known for its colony of artists and wealthy Bostonians escaping the pollution and commotion of the city. Henry David Thoreau and Mark Twain visited the town and its beautiful lake regularly. The school sits on the shoulder of Mount Monadnock, widely believed to be the most climbed mountain in the world. Starting with the Lehmann family, Dublin has made every effort to integrate itself into the Monadnock Region thoughtfully and makes its campus and resources available to the public whenever possible. Dublin students regularly participate in town activities and provide ongoing community service to support people in need.

Working with a school master planner, the board of trustees and administration embarked on an ambitious campus expansion and renovation plan over the last fifteen years. They settled on the cedar-style summer cottages to define the unifying language of the campus and built in local elements to all of their recent projects, including the following new or renovated spaces: The Smith Commons, Programming, Robotics, Imagination, Science and Math Building (PRISM), Cornog Library, Shonk

Recital Hall, Outing Club, Whitney Boathouse, Steel Boathouse, Fletcher Health and Wellness Center, Slopeside Dormitory, Monadnock Dormitory, Fountain Arts Building, Gillespie Arts Building, Head of School House, and Writer's Cabin. Every academic space has been newly built during this period. In the spirit of the Lehmann Family, the school has focused on creating simple and elegant spaces to inspire learning and growth while taking advantage of the campus's beautiful natural setting. Every detail in campus planning focuses on building community, whether it be a fire pit, an inviting common room, a volleyball court, or intersecting paths on the quad.

Dublin makes extensive use of its unique location. Returning to its roots, the school has made a comprehensive effort to build up its year-round trail system. Dublin had some of the earliest ski lifts in the country and now has two handle-tow ski and snowboard lifts with snowmaking and lights. Its internationally recognized Nordic Center has over twenty kilometers of groomed trails with five kilometers of snowmaking and lights. People travel from far and wide to tour and race on the free trail system. There are numerous purpose-built trails for running, mountain biking, snowshoeing, and walking to complement the winter trails. The school recently added a sculpture park on one of its trails. Rowing takes place at a boathouse on Thorndike Lake, where Mount Monadnock provides a stunning backdrop and protection from the prevailing winds. A short walk from campus, Dublin Lake, with its steady winds, and the Whitney Boathouse host the popular sailing team in the fall. The school's two natural grass playing fields and award-winning tennis courts provide stunning views of the surrounding mountains and valleys.

The athletic program takes full advantage of the school's campus, culture, and experienced coaches. Beyond the popular endurance sports offerings (skiing, running, mountain biking, rowing), students join teams for soccer, lacrosse, basketball, sailing, alpine skiing, tennis, snowboarding, and ultimate frisbee. The school finds that the magic of the sports program lies in the mix of beginners, intermediates, and highly experienced athletes it attracts. The culture of trying new things allows students to discover a passion they never knew they had. The experts help the beginners, and today's novice becomes tomorrow's team leader. Every student can play on a varsity team, and they often try many different sports and afternoon arts offerings during their time at Dublin. The approach to athletics supports the school's holistic philosophy, which views the high school years as a time to explore, grow, discover, and expand rather than a time for specialization. Sports also support the school's effort to teach sportsmanship, resilience, teamwork, and composure. Focusing on the process and the growth of its student athletes has led to multiple league, state, and New England Championships in the last ten years.

The performing arts have been a signature program at Dublin for decades. Students can participate in dance as a fall afternoon or year-round evening activity, and theater as a winter activity instead of sports. The annual winter play/musical has become a must-see event in the region. Students are invited to help choreograph scenes in the play, design and build sets, sew costumes, and work on the technological aspects of lighting and sound design. The school believes that the performing arts give students opportunities to find their voice, express themselves in new ways, and learn what it means to be a part of a high-functioning team. It is not uncommon for students to reflect that there are "before and after" moments in the performing arts program and that participating contributes to a larger sense of belonging in the school community.

Dublin has a robust student life program that aims to help students grow smoothly into happy, confident, productive, and responsible young adults. Every student has an advisor, and every advisor meets with their four or five advisees for lunch every week as a group. The faculty finds one-on-one time with their advisee to check in and see how they are doing socially, emotionally, physically, and academically. The Dublin faculty created a list of long-term transfer goals that they hope every student achieves during their time at the school. This list guides the work of the advisor and the student's larger team of adults in the community. These goals include engaging in learning with curiosity and passion, appreciating different perspectives, collaborating for the good of the community, communicating creatively, responding to adversity with resilience, and learning to synthesize and apply knowledge. The advisor is also the primary liaison between the school and the family, checking in with families at least every two weeks.

Dublin recently added a comprehensive wellness program to accompany the construction of its new health and wellness buildings. Students have access to yoga, meditation, and structured, age-appropriate weekly wellness classes covering a range of topics such as nutrition and sex education. Students have daily access to adolescent counselors for either one-off meetings or weekly check-ins. The head of school meets weekly with a CARE Team, composed of various health and wellness stakeholders in the community, to discuss students who are struggling physically or emotionally. The Care Team develops an action plan to collaborate with the students' larger teams and families, providing ongoing structures and strategies to support the students.

Clubs and affinity groups are so crucial to the culture at Dublin that Thursday afternoons are cleared of required activities to make time for student leadership and gatherings. Students work with the dean of students' office to create new clubs and affinity groups. Life in Dublin's seven dormitories is designed to bring students together and learn how to live in community. Weekly milk and cookies conversations help the students get to know one another, and "white glove" cleaning sessions bring about both hesitant groans and team bonding. Students look forward to the annual Dormitory Olympic Games, where both day and boarding students compete in everything from an a cappella singing contest to a dormitory decoration competition.

Dublin School's traditions are designed to amplify and reinforce the community, the mission, and students' sense of belonging. Students regularly rank Winterfest as their favorite school tradition. Winterfest, designed to celebrate living in the mountains in the middle of winter, involves breaking students and faculty into student-led color teams for a weeklong competition. Leading up to the snow games on the weekend, the week is filled with spirit day competitions, highlighted by a boisterous, must-see Friday night lip-sync contest. On Saturday, the parents' association runs a series of winter-themed events, including the human bobsled, snowshoe-nerf biathlon, and tug of war.

Mayfair, a celebration of the arts at Dublin, highlights the spring calendar. Seniors share their senior projects, artists display their visual art and woodworking artifacts in the gallery, dancers perform, and the musicians take center stage for an epic outdoor coffee house. Up to forty different acts perform in a given coffee house, and alumni and alumni parents return in droves to witness the spectacle of students and faculty singing and playing everything from rock to folk to classical to heavy metal music.

Dublin starts every day with perhaps its most important tradition, Morning Meeting. Over two hundred students and staff pour into the Shonk Recital Hall every morning to experience the unexpected, a meeting with no agenda where everyone is invited to participate. Run by the student government, students and faculty line one wall as they wait to take turns sharing an announcement, poem, song, skit, sports update, or presentation. The head of school uses this time to talk about the school's mission, history, values, alumni, future, faculty, and students. Every senior has the opportunity to give a TED Talk-like presentation in Morning Meeting before they graduate. The gathering grounds the community and gives the adults a chance to eyeball their advisees and students before we launch into our separate schedules.

Dublin recently completed a historic campaign for its future, raising its endowment to over $20 million while adding several important buildings and programs to campus. The school received a substantial gift to build a separate outdoor campus on its property, featuring cabins, bathrooms, an amphitheater, a pavilion, and trails, to support its effort to create more screen-free opportunities to spend time in nature. All of these recent developments have helped the school reconnect to its roots and original mission, providing for an adventurous new chapter in the school's history.

Scattergood Friends School

Location: West Branch, Iowa

Year Founded: 1890

Grades Served: 6–8 (Day School), 9–12 (Day & Boarding)

Total Enrollment: 42

Percent Boarding: 60%

Percent Non-White: 18%

Percent From Out of State: 50%

Percent From Out of Country: 10%

2025–26 School Year Tuition: $53,000

Percent Who Receive Financial Aid: 90%

School Website: www.scattergood.org

Head of School: John Zimmerman

Scattergood Friends School

Chapter Completed By

John Zimmerman, Head of School

How do you change the world? Is it through generous philanthropic endeavors, sweeping political movements, or some other grand gesture? At Scattergood Friends School, we believe that the world is shaped one action at a time, every day of our lives, through the choices we make. Each small act contributes to the larger world in which we live and thus every single one of us is both tasked with, and able to, effect the change we would like to see. With a curriculum focused on building life-long learners, Quaker values and practice, and a commitment to living not just off of, but with the land, we prepare students to be successful in their chosen path, but also to scatter good wherever they go, changing the world in the process.

Many who visit Scattergood find themselves adjusting to a different tone, or vibe, than that found at a typical boarding school. The pace of life slows down a bit when you get outside of the major cities and the sprawl of neighborhoods turns into rolling hills and acres of farmland as far as the eye can see. The sense of openness and space lends itself beautifully to a school that places silent reflection and the value of curiosity at its heart. At Scattergood one can take a walk in the prairie, visit the animals at the farm, or take a dip in our pond. There are all sorts of ways to explore and interact with the beautiful nature around us, it is no wonder we begin to slow down and appreciate it.

We are also, however, a place of excitement and intellectual pursuits, brimming with activities and connections to the outside world. Our students bring with them incredible experiences, traditions, and passions that we encourage and support through our curriculum, open workshops and creator spaces on campus, and a curriculum that reflects the passions and interests of our students. With the rich resources of Iowa City and the University of Iowa a short drive, or bike ride, down the road, we are also able to connect with a wide variety of art galleries, theaters, visiting professors, and all that a college town has to offer. Our deep connections to the local community balance the tranquility of rural life and help create that unique blend that is Scattergood Friends School.

Founded in 1890, Scattergood Friends School has served as a boarding school for Quaker and non-Quaker students for much of its history. In the 1930s, the school was closed due to the Great Depression and the impact it had on Midwest farming families. In the 1940s, Iowa Quakers opened the campus up as a hostel for Jewish refugees escaping Europe. At the conclusion of World War II, it was decided to reopen the school and broaden the student body by encouraging non-Quaker students to apply. Since then, Scattergood has welcomed students from all over the world and from a wide variety of backgrounds. Today, we find ourselves at the crossroads of tradition and progress as we seek to carry forward that which has long served students in developing strong values and a deep sense of community, while also meeting the needs of modern students and the expectations of colleges and universities. Through careful design and structure, Scattergood has found that balance.

Since its founding, Scattergood has been a Quaker School, meaning it follows the practices and traditions of the Quaker faith, as practiced in Iowa. This includes a shared set of values called the SPICES – simplicity, peace, integrity, community, equality, and stewardship – daily silent reflection in a group setting, and the belief that there is "that of God" in everyone. These three core aspects of our program are each significant contributors to our end goal of preparing students to help create a more just and sustainable world.

These SPICES serve as a framework for understanding how we are expected to interact with each other, and show up in our daily life. Having a common language to utilize when discussing the complexities of the modern world and the daily struggles we all encounter, provides a path into conversation and understanding for our students. These values also create clear expectations for how our students are expected to think when making choices. Will one's decision lead to a peaceful outcome? Can you achieve your goal with respect for the community? Is leaving that mess really showing good stewardship? And do you have the integrity to answer these questions honestly? These values show up both explicitly and implicitly throughout our academic and community life.

The values of peace and simplicity are, perhaps, best felt when we are engaged in our daily silent reflection. We gather together in the early afternoon for either 15 or 45 minutes of quiet, thoughtful, time together. The Meetinghouse is filled with benches not quite hard enough to cause an ache and not quite soft enough to cause a nap. Students, staff, and guests enter quietly and find a place to sit, often near a friend, but quite often in a space of one's own. Occasionally there is a prompt, or query, or a special activity such as singing or drawing, but most days we simply settle into silence and wait. We don't know exactly what we're waiting for, but every so often, we'll hear it. One of the people in the room will be moved to speak. It's different for everyone, but usually it's a thought that keeps coming back and the sense that others would benefit from hearing it. Sometimes the sharing is a deep philosophical exploration. Sometimes it's a memory triggered by some random inspiration. Sometimes we sit in silence, each person exploring their own imagination, or trying to clear their head, or simply waiting for a staff member to shake hands and thus end the meeting. While this process can be challenging for some people, the exercise is well worth the effort. The advent of smart phones, laptops, and other internet-connected devices has provided us with amazing access to information and entertainment. This same technology also leaves us bereft of opportunities to sit, silently, with our thoughts and reflect upon them, or our day. It is critical that students engage this mental muscle, train it, and learn how to harness the calming, stress-reducing power of giving one's brain time to be still. Many of our students begin their time at Scattergood thinking that they don't want or need to sit quietly each day, but all depart with a deep appreciation for this practice and often seek it in their lives beyond Scattergood.

Finally, the Quaker belief that there is that of God in every person serves as a reminder that each and every student is valuable, capable, and worthy of our time, respect, care, and kindness. To be clear, not every applicant is a fit for every school, and there will always be some students for whom we are not able to meet their particular needs. However, the notion that there is a light, a spark, or whatever term one chooses, inside of each and every student is powerful in its compulsion for us to seek out that light, to nurture that spark, and to avoid the temptation of defining someone by their most challenging of characteristics. In holding our students "in the light" we seek to provide them with support, boundaries, guidance, encouragement, and understanding, so that they may flourish.

Just as our Quaker underpinnings give us a strong foundation, we must also provide students with an academic experience that prepares them for college, career, and a life of learning and growing. Over the past 135 years, Scattergood Friends school has shifted its approach to academics as research, resources, and the ever changing needs of students have grown and progressed. Since the 1970s, that shift has been towards a progressive, student-centered classroom that utilizes group discussions, multi-media presentations, and engaging, hands-on activities. Our campus provides excellent classroom spaces in which students might encounter a variety of vegetation and taste nature's bounty with an informed guide, learn about the importance of prairie fires with a practical demonstration, or experience the birth of a calf or lamb. Our students visit the museums, research centers, and other fascinating resources in Iowa City. Classes at Scattergood provide students with engaging and relevant topics to explore, while ensuring that the skills and base knowledge needed are developed, deepened, and mastered. It is our belief that students who are engaged and interested in their classes are far more likely to engage the material and grow as a student. The academic program at Scattergood provides a wide range of subjects and methodologies for learning, so that every student is able to find out how they best learn and grow in confidence and knowledge.

While it is our academic goal to prepare students for college with traditional academic courses such as Calculus, Physics, and our Junior and Senior term papers, we also want to ensure they are prepared for alternative paths and understand their options. For students with a clear sense of a career path, or a passion they would like to pursue in life, we provide opportunities to work on those plans while still in high school. The Focus Program at Scattergood allows Juniors and Seniors to identify a focus within one of three categories: Arts & Craftsmanship, Sustainable Agriculture, and Peace & Social Transformation. Students in the Focus Program are partnered with mentors and given the opportunity to develop a capstone project. This creates an amazing opportunity for the individual student, but also serves as a point of deliberate reinforcement of our shared values. The capstone projects must include a benefit to our community, or another community, to be approved. This creates a cycle in which students pursue their passion in a way that benefits the community, while also inspiring others to join the program and do the same, leaving their own positive mark on the community. From art installations, to the installation of a mushroom farm, our students have utilized this program to chart a course for their own future, while making the present better for our community.

The word "community" comes up a lot at Scattergood, as it does at many schools. It is clear that having a strong community, in which one can feel welcomed, appreciated, and supported, is vital in the lives of anyone, particularly teenagers. What do we mean, then, when we talk about a school having a good community? What does that feel like, and how does a school nurture and develop a shared experience that promotes interconnectedness?

The SPICES, our shared values, help give Scattergood a clear sense of priorities and expectations for community engagement, and serve as the foundation for building our program. At Scattergood it is clear that everyone is to be treated with respect, that no one is to be othered or made to feel less than. At the same time, we cannot create a space in which feelings will never be hurt, and where everyone shares the same opinion on every topic. Life is messy and conflicts arise. Even something as simple as making a decision on the theme of a dance can lead to emotional turbulence and disagreement. Everyone makes mistakes, and no school is immune to interpersonal drama; the difference is in how one chooses to respond to these moments and whether or not they become moments of growth. There are several ways in which Scattergood prepares students for this aspect of life, both proactively and reactively.

When things go wrong, we don't overreact, we address the issues at hand and move forward. Young people need boundaries. Young people challenge boundaries. The job of a parent, or a boarding staff member acting as a parental stand-in, is to create and reinforce these boundaries in a way that allows a young person to build up the good behavior without becoming entrenched in the us/them dynamic that teenagers often seem hardwired to embrace. Scattergood has developed a system in which staff track student behaviors and engage in conversations aimed at understanding and providing support to help a student live into the expectation that was missed. This Daily Expectations System allows students to see the impact of their actions, and to process how to address correcting these mistakes, without the need to assign arbitrary consequences or build a resistance to receiving feedback. There are, of course, certain behaviors that require explicit boundaries and consequences. Even in those instances, we strive to respond in a way that both reinforces our school expectations and boundaries, while providing students with the help and support they need. Through this restorative approach, Scattergood is able to create a culture in which students trust staff and recognize that mistakes can be learned from and moved past, while knowing that truly egregious behaviors will not be tolerated, something all students appreciate and feel comfort in knowing.

But even better than reacting to things going wrong, is creating systems and routines that help ensure that things go right. One such aspect of Scattergood life is our Crew program. There is no janitorial staff that comes in at night to clean up. Instead, we take responsibility, as a community, for maintaining our campus. Each student and staff member is assigned a crew, with students rotating through crews and staff leading a consistent task throughout the year. Crews range from restoring classrooms to collecting recyclables, to feeding the farm animals, to cleaning up after lunch. Each crew serves a vital function in our daily life and helps students grow in a variety of ways. First, every crew imparts a new, valuable skill upon a student. Many students arrive at Scattergood having never mopped, done the dishes, or perhaps even having never done chores at all. When students learn how to do these things, they gain confidence in their ability to handle other physical tasks, to work with their body as well as their mind, and to acquire a skill that might come in handy somewhere down the line. Students also develop an appreciation for working in partnership with others to accomplish a shared goal. New students on meal cleanup sometimes ask, "when is this crew down?" The answer, of course, is, "whenever we are done." This is often an epiphany of sorts for the student as they begin to realize that their level of effort and willingness to be an engaged crew member directly impacts how long it will take for them, and everyone else, to finish. As students spend more time on crew, they begin to find the joy in this kind of work and share music, stories, and laughter while working and building relationships. Sure, we could hire a janitorial staff, but why would we want to?

Crew can be challenging, but that's just one more reason to do it. In fact, at Scattergood, we believe it is our job to set up all sorts of challenges for our students. Students are not fragile beings that will wilt or shatter when asked to go outside their comfort zones. They are, instead, "anti-fragile," like the muscles in our bodies, or our immune system. Each challenge, provided it is appropriate and not harmful, provides an opportunity to grow stronger and more resilient. Each task that seems out of reach, that a student then grasps and holds, encourages them to challenge themselves further. To that end, we do not shy away from asking students to stretch themselves and try new things. The two-night fall camping trip challenges those who have never slept in a tent, or discovered the charm of a campsite restroom. Having had a fun time on the fall trip, a student might sign up for a week-long camping trip, or perhaps a hiking trip. With those skills under their belt, perhaps a student will be inspired to take on the challenge of a three-week long canoe trip or journey along the Appalachian trail, or a service trip to Latin America.

Perhaps the most unique aspect of our program, and one of the most important, is the Scattergood approach to meetings and decision making. Inspired by the Quaker Meeting for Business, Scattergood students and staff hold a number of weekly meetings that focus on various aspects of community life. Each meeting is organized by a pair of clerks, often students, who set the agenda and help keep things moving. While there are some decisions that must be made by the Head of School, or a department chair, or some other small group, whenever possible, school decisions are made in these group settings. Any student or staff may bring an item to the clerks and, more often than not, that item will appear on a subsequent meeting's agenda. These items can include establishing or changing a rule, new initiatives or events, or topics of concern. A recent topic of concern on the subject of cell phones led to several community-wide conversations that ultimately led to a change in policy and the creation of a revised, phone-free school day. In these meetings, all are free to speak and the item will continue until there is a sense of the meeting, that is, a shared path forward that all are able to accept. This process may be lengthier than simply voting, but it allows for all voices to be heard, and for everyone to feel comfortable with the final outcome. Often the time spent in conversation is saved in execution as the process leads to greater buy-in up front, and less resistance to the next steps.

The world is not changed in a single moment, even though it often feels that way. Each "moment" is the result of a series of decisions and interactions that shape the world and create the conditions for those inflection points that turn history. At Scattergood we have crafted a program that builds life-long learners who possess a deep appreciation for hard work, listening, and building consensus. Our students understand the impact of their choices on the community and world around them. We instill students with a strong sense of values and the tools needed to reflect on their lives and the challenges they face and they sort out how to maintain those values while moving forward. Scattergood is preparing students to change the world one day, one task, one interaction at a time. By planting themselves in our fertile soil, students grow and leave our campus prepared to scatter good wherever they go.

Solebury School

Location: New Hope, Pennsylvania

Year Founded: 1925

Grades Served: 9–12 + Post Grad

Total Enrollment: 260

Percent Boarding: 48%

Percent Non-White: 33%

Percent From Out of State: 80%

Percent From Out of Country: 12%

2025–26 School Year Tuition: $74,555

Percent Who Receive Financial Aid: 45%

School Website: www.solebury.org

Head of School: Tom Wilschutz

Solebury School

Chapter Completed By

Scott Eckstein, Director of Enrollment Management and Financial Aid

Let's make a school that is different, where students love learning.

It was 1925, and that was the sentiment that drove Solebury School's founders. They were young teachers working at traditional New England boarding schools as well as at an overnight camp in New Hampshire. They found life at camp full of camaraderie, learning, and adventure, whereas school almost seemed to require teachers and students to leave these qualities at the door. As founder Laurie Erskine wrote, school was too often "a decidedly depressing and boring experience for all students (which) frustrated really talented teachers who would have liked to excite in their students a lively and comprehensive interest in their subjects." Their goal was to have students held to high standards of achievement, but in an atmosphere that maintained the joy, the openness, and the friendliness of the camp where they spent their summers.

They sought to establish a progressive and collaborative school, one which was not bound by convention. They were dedicated to nurturing students who could think and strove to create an environment where everyone felt included.

Now enjoying its second century of giving this experience to students, Solebury School remains true to this founding ideal. It is a place whose essence is easy to see and feel, and whose spirit fosters a profoundly impactful experience for its students and faculty.

The spirit is partly fueled by the school's location in New Hope, Pennsylvania. A small town halfway between New York City and Philadelphia, New Hope is a historic and artistic community. It is a place known for its beautiful landscapes, for its rolling hills and sprawling farmland, and for being a charming town on the Delaware River just 20 minutes from where Washington crossed on a cold night during the Revolutionary War. Long known as a haven for painters, playwrights, novelists and actors, it is home to the Bucks County Playhouse, whose stage has featured Robert Redford, Angela Lansbury, Alan Alda, Liza Minelli, and many other famous performers in its long history. It is a place where people from New York and Philadelphia have come for decades to recharge. The school's location allows its students and staff to have both the safety and peace of a small town and the vibrancy of two urban centers.

Solebury was founded to be a small school – one that believed in the power of close connection between students and between students and teachers. This belief, that connection is what can unlock our potential in all areas of life, is the foundational value of Solebury. As Erskine described:

> *The key to satisfying an adolescent's love of learning was nothing more nor less than a frank and honest friendship between the teachers and his pupils... A friendship which evokes good faith from the youth and from the adult a respect for the adolescent's sincere desire to learn.*

These close, working relationships continue to be at the center of school life and to drive the other core tenets of the school. They are the heart of the joyful, supportive, intellectual community that exists today.

Once upon a time, four young teachers wondered whether school could be better. One hundred years later, Solebury School continues to demonstrate that the answer is "yes."

A Down-to-Earth Place

Physically, culturally, and spiritually, Solebury is a down-to-earth place, one that is uninterested in any form of pretension. The 140-acre campus is an old farm – the Main Office is the original farmhouse, the Theater is in the original barn. The campus has expanded during the school's history as new facilities have been built, but the open space, the creek and pond, and the architecture, continue to evoke the feeling of being on a bucolic farm. There are enormous oaks and sycamores everywhere you look, and there are a bevy of trails to walk on while contemplating a book, a math problem, or life in general.

From the school's beginning and continuing to today, many classrooms at Solebury open directly to the outdoors, requiring students to step outside between classes. On almost any day, students can be found at the outdoor tables or in the Adirondack chairs throughout the property doing schoolwork or just enjoying each other's company. This is a defining feature of the campus experience. The constant exposure to fresh air and the natural surroundings, with easy access to trees and open sky, has nurtured generations of students, fostering a unique connection between learning and the environment. As Evie '25 put it,

> *When I think of the Solebury community, it's impossible to separate my connection to students and staff from the connection we foster with the space itself. In the winter, we rush outdoors between classes to savor the early sprinklings of snow. When May arrives, we pick strawberries in the*

community garden and eat in the sun below blooming trees. A Solebury education – and social experience – is completely tied to our surroundings and the beauty of the campus.

This down-to-earth quality can also be seen in the way students and faculty dress. There is no dress code at Solebury School; it is a place designed for people to be themselves, to feel comfortable and confident in how they present themselves to the world. These presentations run the gamut – from students who look like they stepped out of a trendy fashion catalog, to those who present more formally, to those who wear shorts all winter. While Solebury is not a place where anything goes, it prefers to focus on what matters. It believes that conversations between staff and students lead to better outcomes and, ultimately, to more maturity, than do picayune rules about how tucked-in a shirt needs to be. The school's most important injunction to students is that they "show up and be ready." This means being alert, prepared, and open to learning. If a student feels best doing this in a sweatshirt, so be it! For Solebury, seriousness of purpose comes from inside of a person, and not from the clothes they wear.

Finally, this lack of pretension can be observed in the way the faculty and students interact. Students call staff by their first names. This reflects the idea that the faculty are people students can engage with and talk to – that they are not simply bastions of authority, that they can be questioned. This idea of a mutual, authentic respect between teachers and students is central to the school. Students do not respect teachers based on simply their age or their title. The respect comes from a shared purpose, from a genuine knowledge each has of the other, from the friendship that Laurie Erskine emphasized at the school's founding.

Solebury truly sees students – their talents, their potential, and their full humanity. It has always been a leader in welcoming students. It was one of the first coed secondary schools, one of the first schools to welcome students of color, and it has been a leader in welcoming students of different gender identities. To be able to come as you are, and to have that be valued and understood, is core to the Solebury experience.

A School That Says "Yes"

The comfort that students feel – on the campus, as individuals who are seen and known, and in their relationships with faculty – leads to a deep confidence. It leads to a sense that they, and their ideas, are of worth. In turn, this leads to a willingness to speak and to question. As Orly '27 said, "Our teachers at Solebury teach with curiosity, not judgment. They encourage students to not passively accept information and ideas, but rather to examine and search for truth." Students know they have a voice, that what they say is taken seriously. This voice enables them to advocate for themselves and for the community as a whole. They debate in class, they propose a club or a new program, and they are active in helping the school evolve and in shaping their years here. Solebury honors this by trying to say yes.

You want to dig deeply into areas of passion? Solebury has developed Academic Concentrations in STEM, Social Justice, Global Education, or Arts and Letters for you to do so. They'll support your independent study on entrepreneurship to help you launch a business, on developing a non-profit to combat human trafficking, or on the engineering and physics behind automobile design. They'll form a partnership with a professional dance studio to allow you to have a high level academic program and a Conservatory experience. Want to create an art installation or produce your own concert or performance? Solebury will say, "Let's pick a date." You have an idea for an improved student cafe? The administration will help you develop a plan, obtain resources, and make it happen. Whereas students at many schools are dragged along by an unrelenting current, Solebury encourages students to grab an oar and help steer their experience and the school as a whole.

All of this is what makes Solebury students particularly able to take on that which is hard and to have the confidence that they can navigate it. It is easier to confront challenges when you know there are people behind you, believing in you and cheering you on.

A living example of all this is Juli '20, who arrived at Solebury with a passion for the environment and sustainable development. She completed Solebury's Global Education concentration and pushed Solebury to do more to meet the UN's Sustainable Development Goals. The school listened and made several changes based on her thoughts. Her experiences during her time at Solebury have launched her career in the non-profit sector.

Amplifying Curiosity and Fostering Discovery

The empowerment students feel, the agency they develop, and the wide range of academic and extracurricular options available to them amplify the natural curiosity that exists in young people. Solebury students live and learn in a schedule designed deliberately to allow for extensive intellectual exploration, engagement in creative endeavors, and a balanced life. Students have three academic classes each day, with each of their subjects meeting for 80 minutes every other day. This allows classes to delve deeper, to focus on dynamic, hands-on learning, and to give space for the kind of inquiry that is a hallmark of a Solebury education. Students might find themselves performing a scene from *Macbeth* and then dissecting it. They might work on a plan to synthesize the best aspects of various societies throughout history and create their version of a utopia. They might build a drone from scratch.

The schedule also contains a dedicated arts block where students can select from a staggering variety of arts electives ranging from traditional visual arts to metalworking, from engineering to dance, from rock band to bookmaking, from lighting design to video game design. These creative endeavors are seen as equally valuable to traditional intellectual pursuits. The protected arts block in the schedule allows for students to have significant experience in, and exploration of, the arts without sacrificing their pursuit of the other academic realms. These artistic pursuits expand students' minds, and they enhance their work in other disciplines. They make students better mathematicians, writers, and linguists, better historians, readers, and scientists.

Looking at the course catalog, one could easily think it was from a small college rather than a small boarding school. In addition to the core curriculum, students can take classes such as Microbiology, Literature of the Underworld, Ornithology, Debating the Civil Rights Movement through Film, Cybersecurity, and The Story of Food: Reading, Writing, Eating. Solebury's environment, culture, and program embrace and encourage curiosity – of oneself and one's potential, of others, of ideas and subjects, and of the world.

As students explore, they will find a curriculum that will meet them where they are. For some students, a full slate of Honors and AP classes is what is right. Others benefit from our Learning Support Programs to figure out how to bridge the gap between their natural intelligence and their skills as a student. Others need a combination of these things – the academic challenge of high level classes and the support to navigate them as successfully as possible. As students stretch themselves, their sense of what they are capable of expands, and they discover the joy that comes from finding where their talent and their interests intersect.

The same is true extracurricularly. As part of a small student body, Solebury students are immediately and consistently able to be part of a team, to join a club, to try new things, and to discover interests and talents that were previously unknown. Athletes who are devoted to a sport can find a home alongside those who discover a passion for athleticism or who meet their best friends through the camaraderie of teamwork. If a team sport isn't your thing, you can choose from the host of other after school activity options to enjoy. You can be part of the tremendous theater or theater tech programs where thespians bound for acting programs in college perform alongside those who previously only sang in the shower. Those who prefer to be behind the scenes get the incredible experience of working in Solebury's black box theater – creating the stage and the set specifically for each show and using the professional light and sound systems to hone their craft. Traditional shows like *Rent* share the stage with more avant garde offerings like *Evil Dead*. Students can also participate in a non-competitive physical activity like rock climbing or yoga, or find community and shared joy in an activity like Debate, Model UN, E-sports, or Dungeons and Dragons. While there are plenty of students whose love for a subject or an activity only grows deeper and more profound during their years on campus, it is also common to find the singer who discovers they can throw the discus, the basketball player who finds they are great with a camera, and the history buff whose eyes are opened to the beauty of math.

A graduate of the Class of '24, Maggie's years at Solebury illustrate this beautifully. During her time at Solebury, she had an academic schedule full of AP classes, but also took over 20 art classes. She thrived across the academic program and also proposed doing a mural which now enhances the beauty of campus. Finally, when giving a speech at graduation, she discussed how she learned to be open to a classmate whose beliefs were diametrically opposite of her own and how this not only made her a better student, but also a better human being.

Growth

Solebury's culture and program thus lead to significant growth in all realms – intellectual, extracurricular, and personal. This can happen in countless ways. It can be the student who was a high flier in middle school who learns to soar to new heights. Or the student who prior schools tried to rein in and put in a box who finally is able to unleash all their talents. It can be the introvert who finds the confidence to stand up and make an announcement during the student-led, all-school assemblies. Or the student whose mind is opened by going to school with people from varied backgrounds and walks of life. It can be the student who discovers the satisfaction of managing things away from their parents – taking care of their business, advocating for themselves, and navigating the highs and lows of life. Or the student who dedicates themselves to a craft and nurtures potential into remarkable performance. Solebury's students are excited by their intellectual and personal development, and continuously grow to recognize their own capacity to do extraordinary things.

As Alex '14 put it,

> *Before Solebury, there were different versions of myself in different situations. There was Alex with my parents, Alex with my friends, Alex in the classroom... Solebury allowed me to be myself in all of these situations – one true, authentic Alex, and to fully appreciate what I was capable of in all areas of life.*

One way this growth is fostered is by Solebury's willingness to give students some control over their time. After all, nothing is more important in preparing students for college and for life than learning how to make choices about how to use and control time. Solebury believes that one cannot learn to manage time unless they have some time to manage. As such, most students have some free time in their day – an intentional choice to help them learn to decide when they need to write up their lab report for AP Chemistry and when they can go to the school cafe with a friend. Within the structure of the daily schedule and evening programming, students are able to develop this skill on a daily basis.

This ability to make choices combines with the freedom students enjoy – of thought, of endeavor, and of expression – to allow students to develop their own path and to maximize their overall development. Driven by their own genuine excitement and the connection they feel with their teachers, students go farther than they thought they could.

This growth is embodied by the story of J.R. '16. He arrived at Solebury as a shy 14-year-old, having been bullied at his previous school due to his stutter. However, even before the end of 9th grade, he began making announcements in the All-School Assemblies about service projects he was passionate about. He eventually went on to become School President, and his empathy and intelligence combined to make him a force here and beyond.

Me As Part of Us

Solebury encourages all its students (and faculty) to view their individual growth, their individual selves, and their individual endeavors within the context of the larger community. How do I fit within the group? How do I contribute to the whole? This idea, that all students and faculty are important to the functioning of the school, is reinforced by an egalitarian approach to various pursuits. Whereas at many schools, athletics dominate the culture, this is not so at Solebury. The students in the theater tech program are just as valued by the school and by their peers as the captains of the athletic teams. Those who dream of a career in coding appreciate the passion of those who dream of a career in law and vice versa. Students turn out to support each other's efforts. They scream from the bleachers at basketball games, give standing ovations at sold-out theater performances, and give heartfelt snaps at the annual poetry slam. Students appreciate that all these pursuits take dedication, courage, and strength of character. Solebury fervently lives the idea that there can only be a true community when all students and their interests are regarded as equally valuable.

Students learn that the joy they feel when pursuing the things that excite them is enhanced when it is shared. They see that their work hits new levels when supported by peers and that they have the potential to do this for others. Cultivating this sense of interconnectedness is central to the Solebury ethos. It is the responsibility of each member of the community to discover what they do best and to pursue it with vigor so that they are adding to the whole as much as possible. Simultaneously, it is the responsibility of each member of the community to help others grow and be their best in and out of the classroom. The whole is truly greater than the sum of its parts.

A student who reflects this aspect of Solebury is Terrance '21. Terrance joined Solebury thinking of himself primarily as a basketball player. He saw the work his friends were putting into rehearsing for plays and began going to support them. Soon, he began going to every performance of every play. Eventually, he decided to leave the audience and become part of a cast himself.

Ready For the World

All of the core elements of Solebury School help students become better humans who are equipped to enter a changing, wondrous, and complex world. When students are able to learn and grow in a down-to-earth environment that nurtures their curiosity and says "yes" to their ideas, all while helping them develop their sense of independence and balance the recognition of their individuality with the power of community... magic happens.

Thus, students do not leave Solebury simply as better mathematicians or musicians, philosophers or physicists, polyglots or poets. They graduate as thoughtful, informed, empathetic, and open-minded people. They graduate with an understanding of the complex world we live in and the various ways they might positively impact it. They leave Solebury with an understanding of themselves and their potential, and ready to tackle whatever comes next.

Interlochen Arts Academy

Location: Interlochen, Michigan

Year Founded: 1962

Grades Served: 9–12 + Post Grad

Total Enrollment: 577

Percent Boarding: 92%

Domestic Diversity: 36%

Percent From Out of State: 78%

Percent From Out of Country: 17%

2025–26 School Year Tuition: $78,725

Percent Who Receive Financial Aid: 83%

School Website: www.interlochen.org

Head of School: Trey Devey, President; Dr. Camille Colatosti, Provost

Interlochen Arts Academy

Chapter Completed By
Maureen Oleson, Director of Communications

Creating a Place for Young Artists

Founded in 1962 by pioneering music educator Dr. Joseph Maddy, Interlochen Arts Academy is the nation's first – and foremost – fine arts-focused boarding high school.

The Academy was the continuation of Maddy's lifelong efforts to advance music education at the high school level. A professional musician-turned educator, Maddy was one of the first individuals in U.S. history to hold the position of music supervisor for a public school system. In 1926, Maddy was asked to assemble an ensemble of the finest young orchestral musicians from across the country to perform at the Music Supervisors National Conference in Detroit, Michigan. The resulting ensemble, known as the National High School Orchestra, featured 232 high school musicians from 25 U.S. states.

The remarkable success of the inaugural National High School Orchestra inspired Maddy to create a place where gifted young musicians could rehearse and perform under the guidance of acclaimed instructors, not just for a week, but for an entire summer. In 1928, he welcomed 115 students to the inaugural season of the National High School Orchestra Camp (known today as Interlochen Arts Camp).

While Interlochen began as an orchestra- and band-focused camp, it soon embraced other artistic and musical disciplines. The Camp introduced a choral program and staged its first operetta, *The Pirates of Penzance*, in 1929. New arts programs were added to meet student interest and recognize the interrelated nature of art. Visual arts and theatre were added in 1939; dance followed a year later in 1940.

By the 1950s, Maddy's Camp had grown exponentially – as had his aspirations. Maddy began actively working toward his next dream: A year-round boarding high school where artistically gifted students could pursue exceptional academic coursework alongside conservatory-caliber arts training. Throughout the 1950s, Maddy winterized a number of his Camp's existing facilities and added new buildings to support the new school, including an administration building, two dormitories, and a student center. Interlochen Arts Academy officially opened in 1962 with 132 students studying classical music, theatre, dance, and visual arts.

Over the years, the Academy has expanded its curriculum to include training in creative writing (1976), film and new media (2005), interdisciplinary arts (2009), and multiple areas of contemporary music, including jazz (1972), singer-songwriter (2012), and music production and engineering (2019). Today, the Academy is widely regarded as the premier boarding arts high school in the nation and has a proven record of preparing students for exceptional careers in the arts and beyond. Academy students routinely win top prizes in nationally recognized youth arts competitions, such as the Scholastic Art & Writing Awards, YoungArts, and the Youth America Grand Prix. The Academy has produced two National Student Poets and 51 Presidential Scholars in the Arts – more than any other high school in the nation.

A Haven Between the Lakes

Maddy's vision for his Camp always included a healthy balance of artistic rigor and outdoor recreation – all set against an inspiring backdrop of natural splendor. After a nationwide search for an idyllic "artist's haven," Maddy found the perfect site in Interlochen, Michigan.

Nestled between two pristine lakes, Interlochen's forested, 1,200-acre campus continues to be a source of reflection and rejuvenation and a defining characteristic of the Camp and Academy experience. More than 400 buildings dot the campus – from rustic practice cabins and historic amphitheaters to state-of-the-art artistic facilities. Notable structures include the 4,000-seat, open-air Kresge Auditorium; the Alden Dow-designed academic rotundas; and a robust music library that contains one of the world's largest collections of performing ensemble literature.

Each of Interlochen's seven artistic disciplines has its own designated space on campus – all meticulously designed with the division's unique needs in mind. Two of these artistic "homes," The Writing House and the DeRoy Center for Film Studies, were the first structures in the nation dedicated to the study of creative writing and film, respectively, at the high school level. The Music Center is home to the school's largest artistic division. The 60,000 square-foot facility features two rehearsal halls; two recording studios; 11 ensemble rooms; 10 practice rooms; 26 private lesson teaching studios; and an onsite instrument repair shop. The architecture award-winning Dance Center seamlessly combines the historic Hildegarde Lewis Dance Building with the new Nancy Hoagland Wing to create 25,000 square feet of light-filled, professional-quality studio spaces overlooking Green Lake.

Protecting northern Michigan's natural resources has been a priority at Interlochen since the Camp's earliest days. The institution's Sustainability Team leads efforts to foster an ecologically friendly environment and educate students on the importance of sustainable living. The R.B. Annis Botanical Lab and Community Garden serves as a hub for the school's sustainability education efforts – which include semester-long, for-credit courses for Academy students. In 2019, Interlochen Arts Academy was recognized as a U.S. Department of Education Green Ribbon School.

Conservatory-Caliber Training – at the High School Level

> *My time at Interlochen strongly influenced both my personal and artistic development. Being surrounded by peers and faculty, all devoted artists; spending countless hours diving deeply into new concepts in critiques; and maintaining my personal practice have all made for a challenging and amazing four years.*
>
> – Maud, Academy student

The arts program is the defining characteristic of the Interlochen Arts Academy experience: Every student spends approximately four hours per day immersed in the art form of their choice. Arts classes are taught by dedicated artist-educators with decades of real-world experience as performers and professionals within their respective disciplines.

The Academy offers training in seven art forms – Creative Writing, Dance, Film & New Media, Interdisciplinary Arts, Music, Theatre, and Visual Arts – with a variety of specializations available within the school's larger artistic divisions.

Creative Writing

The Creative Writing major nurtures young writers' talent, stimulates their imagination, and broadens their command of the writer's craft. Fiction, poetry, and nonfiction workshops form the core of the program; students also engage in a variety of electives. Proficiency in a broad range of genres builds versatility and control, preparing students for the rigors of college-level work as well as publication. Through individualized mentorship and intensive workshops, students develop an awareness of their strengths and challenges, while expanding their patience and self-discipline. Students leave the program with a portfolio of carefully revised work in a variety of genres.

Dance

The Dance major offers pre-professional training to instill the discipline and skill necessary to pursue dance at premier higher education programs and as a career. Academy dancers study both classical and contemporary dance. Students spend three to five hours per day in classes such as classical ballet technique, pointe, *pas de deux*, character dance, contemporary, jazz, hip-hop, and other genres. The program places a strong emphasis on rehearsing for public performances, including full-length ballets. Academy dancers have regular opportunities to audition for college and university programs, professional companies, and summer intensives.

Film and New Media

In the Film & New Media major, students learn the art and craft of storytelling and multimedia production through critical studies and hands-on experience. The curriculum guides students through progressive, interdisciplinary, and collaborative courses in digital video, screenwriting, film history, and related arts. Students also have the opportunity to explore game design, animation, and new media creation. Screenwriting workshops help students develop storytelling skills and learn the narrative structure of a film. Production classes explore the visual and aural aspects of filmmaking, such as cinematography, lighting, music, sound, directing, and editing. Electives from other arts majors expand students' appreciation of the components that make up a film. Students graduate with strong experience in writing, producing, directing, and editing their own projects.

Interdisciplinary Arts

The Interdisciplinary Arts major attracts young artists with skills and interests in multiple artistic disciplines. With a curriculum designed to accommodate exploration across arts areas, students participate in a daily studio class as well as core classes in contemporary arts performance and culture, arts leadership/management, and portfolio development. Independent studies, collaborative projects, individual studio time, arts electives, and guest artist instruction are also key components of the Interdisciplinary Arts major. Students may choose to participate in the Interdisciplinary Performance Collaboration, a year-long course open to all majors and grade levels that culminates in an original presentation in the spring. Through an innovative curriculum, interdisciplinary arts students pursue their individual artistic interests and develop vital leadership skills while cultivating a uniquely informed passion for the arts.

Music

The classical music program, which offers a choice of performance and composition tracks, prepares students for the rigors of study at the university and conservatory level. Advanced music theory classes and weekly private lessons prepare students to put their skills into practice in a variety of ensembles, including orchestra, wind symphony, chamber singers, choir, brass choir, and more. These ensembles have a global reputation for excellence, serving as reading ensembles for composition students and enabling performance students to develop concert experience and sight-reading skills, as well as knowledge of a diverse and challenging repertoire.

The contemporary music program imparts the skills aspiring musicians need to thrive in the commercial music industry. Students pursue a well-rounded curriculum that provides instruction in both the technical and business aspects of life as a contemporary musician. Students can choose from several tracks, including popular performance, jazz performance, and singer-songwriter.

Music Production & Engineering students work directly and collaboratively with artists, composers, songwriters, musicians, and other engineers, designers, and producers to create high-quality recording and technology projects in a professional production environment. Students explore current practices and innovations in music technology, using digital audio workstations including Pro Tools, Ableton, and Logic. They learn electronic musicianship, music production, and key aspects of recording and production – from recording session set-up and microphone placement to signal flow and mix-down. Additionally, students master professional studio protocol and develop critical listening skills, as well as the aesthetic, communication, and organizational competencies vital to successful producers and engineers.

Theatre

The Theatre major challenges students to develop both individually and within an ensemble. Students can focus their studies in acting, musical theatre, or design and production, while gaining exposure in all mediums. Acting at Interlochen is Stanislavski-based with a focus on inner truth. Students explore a wide range of genres, including classical text, acting for the camera, and contemporary theatre, in addition to audition preparation.

The musical theatre track focuses on acting, with expanded skill development in singing, movement, and sequential dance training.

The design and production concentration enables students to perceive, visualize, and realize practical designs for the theatre. The track offers pre-professional training in multiple aspects of technical theatre, including scenic, lighting, costume, and sound design.

Visual Arts

The Visual Arts major develops a young artist's technical and conceptual abilities through an integrated curriculum that fosters connections between disciplines and media. By encouraging creative practices, such as flexible thinking, inquisitiveness, and perseverance, the Academy program lays the foundation for a deeper understanding of arts and innovation. Students develop advanced technical skills in multi-dimensional forms through daily study and practice of diverse media including painting, sculpting, printmaking, digital arts, and more. Regular critiques refine personal vision within a tight-knit artistic community. Visual artists at Interlochen gain the confidence and empathy to develop as citizen artists and leaders.

From Interlochen to the World

> *I am so proud of how this experience improved not only my artistic skill, but also my integrity and determination towards working in a community-based setting. I have never experienced so much support, hard work, and most importantly, so much fun. The connection and friendships that bonded through this experience truly made me re-establish why I love music and further confirmed that I am on the right path with my career.*
>
> – Audrey, Academy student

For students considering a career in the arts, few experiences are more valuable than getting a firsthand look at life as a working artist. As a result, touring opportunities are a key component of Interlochen's arts program.

Each year, students embark on a wide range of local, regional, national, and international tours. The school has established artistic partnerships with The Philadelphia Orchestra and Boston Symphony Orchestra which include opportunities for students to perform side-by-side with members of both ensembles in the orchestras' home venues. Theatre students premiered *Brave Irene* to the Edinburgh Festival Fringe. Piano students recently performed in Carnegie Hall. Members of the school's singer-songwriter program have the chance to participate in an annual tour to musical hotbeds across the country. Animation students regularly attend the Ottawa International Animation Festival in Ottawa, Canada. Film students attended the SXSW Film & TV Festival for the world premiere of *Jedo's Dead* – an award-winning short film they helped create. Music Production & Engineering students have toured professional studios in California and Nashville. Dance students have partnered with Martha Graham Dance Company; performed at the Joyce Theater; and brought full-length ballet productions to venues across northern Michigan.

Every other year, nearly one-quarter of the Academy's student body departs for a national tour. These high-profile events enable students to explore and perform in leading cultural destinations such as New York City, Miami, Chicago, Detroit, and Washington, D.C.

Each major trip culminates with a performance at one of the nation's most prestigious venues. The centerpiece of these events is often a multidisciplinary work such as *MUKTI* – an original production created by students and performed side-by-side with members of the New York Philharmonic.

Beyond touring opportunities, Academy students interface with the world's leading artists through a robust visiting artist program. More than 100 guest artists in all artistic disciplines visit campus each year to lead master classes, serve as competition judges, and collaborate with students. Recent guests include choreographer and author Twyla Tharp; composers Reena Esmail and Chen Yi; pianist Jeremy Denk; *SEAL Team* actor Toni Trucks; playwright Sue Pak; *New York Times* bestselling author Mona Awad; New York City Ballet Director of Repertoire Craig Hall; museum consultants Elaine Gurian and James Volkert; Academy Award-nominated director and animator Troy Quane, among many others.

Academics for artists

> *Interlochen has been transformational for [our son]... Being in an academic environment with other creative problem-solvers has shown him that a non-traditional approach can produce superior results.*
>
> – Caty and Robert, Academy parents

Since its inception, Interlochen Arts Academy has embraced a bold philosophy: That arts and academics do not compete with, but rather complement, each other. Students engage in a rigorous college-preparatory academic curriculum alongside unparalleled artistic training – preparing them to excel in any field.

Academics at Interlochen are taught through the lens of the arts, allowing students to explore the rich connections between artistry and intellect. Faculty often incorporate the arts into their lessons, challenging students to discover the physics of string instruments or the historical context behind famous works of art, music, or literature. In addition to traditional subjects such as French, World History, or Geometry, students can also enroll in specialized, arts-centric courses such as Writing About the Arts; History, Research, and Film; and Social Justice, Humanities, and the Arts.

Beyond its own robust catalog of classes, the Academy provides a variety of opportunities for students to pursue advanced academic coursework. The school has partnered with Indiana University's Advance College Project to offer a number of classes – taught on campus by Interlochen instructors – for which students receive both high school and college credit. A vast array of State of Michigan-accredited programs, including AP courses, is available through the school's partnership with Michigan Virtual. High-achieving students can also work with their academic advisors to enroll in virtual programs from some of the nation's top colleges – such as Indiana University High School Online, Northwestern University Center for Talent Development, Johns Hopkins Center for Talented Youth, Brigham Young University Independent Study, and Rice University Visiting Students Program.

A holistic approach to creative youth development

> *What Interlochen provides is more than just a good education – its students receive transformative, often life-changing artistic and personal enrichment, a clarifying and empowering start to a young person's life, regardless of what fields they ultimately pursue.*
>
> – Kurtis, Academy parent

In 2020, Interlochen Arts Academy sought to identify the qualities that define an Interlochen education. After extensive discussions with alumni, faculty, students, and parents, the institution unveiled The Interlochen 5 –

a social-emotional learning program designed to help the next generation of creative changemakers thrive in an increasingly complex world.

Across artistic, academic, and residential learning, students cultivate five core capacities, which prepare them to thrive in the arts and beyond:

Mindfulness, Wellness, and Resilience

Artists require a balance of focus and freedom. The ability to "center," "flow," or be "in the zone" enhances creative performance. The life of an artist is also challenging and frequently on public display, requiring high levels of tenacity and resilience. Developing this capacity is of lifelong value and enhances all of the other capacities of The Interlochen 5.

Creative Capacity

In a world of rapid automation and artificial intelligence, creative capacity is increasingly critical across all professions. Academy students master the underlying principles of creativity and design thinking and learn to apply this mindset to all aspects of their lives.

Interdisciplinary Perspective and Collaboration

Effective, daily collaboration in the classroom and across seven arts majors draws the best from each individual to achieve something no one person can accomplish on their own. Drawing connections across artistic disciplines and other fields of discovery becomes the basis for breakthrough ideas.

Global and Cultural Perspective

Global art and global issues are central to the Academy experience. On this diverse and international campus, students develop a deeper and more direct understanding of different cultures and experiences, developing the character and empathy to thrive in an interconnected world.

Community and Citizen Artistry

Community is at the heart of Interlochen Arts Academy. Citizen artistry extends this concept as students develop, present, and teach art in service to others. The school asks its students to take an active role in building a healthy community, laying the foundation for a lifetime of rewarding and purposeful engagement.

Forging Connections on the Stage and Beyond

Interlochen Arts Academy's traditions offer rich opportunities to share the arts, bond with peers, and connect with the greater northern Michigan community.

Each academic year begins with House Clash, a friendly competition among the Academy's seven residence halls that features events ranging from athletic competitions to rock, paper, scissors battles. Students also join their peers for class trips throughout northern Michigan; senior and postgraduate students enjoy a highly anticipated trip to nearby Mackinac Island.

Artistic performances form a significant portion of the Academy's traditions. "Collage," the Academy's annual multidisciplinary showcase, unites students from all artistic disciplines for a whirlwind tour of the arts. Students celebrate the holiday season with a full-length production of *The Nutcracker* and the perennial audience favorite, Sounds of the Season. Winterlochen, the school's winter festival, invites local families to campus to enjoy a wide variety of free activities – including outdoor fun, arts-based activities, and a family-friendly performance. The year concludes with

Festival, a three-day event that features dozens of student performances, screenings, readings, and exhibitions.

Other end-of-the-year events include Street Beat – an outdoor carnival on the school's Osterlin Mall – and Interlochen's version of prom, MORP.

Leading lives of service and significance

After Interlochen, graduates matriculate to the nation's finest colleges and conservatories – and from there, to decorated careers in every field imaginable. Interlochen alumni hold principal chairs in major orchestras, serve as artistic directors of dance and theatre companies, star on Broadway and television, and pursue careers in law, medicine, engineering, politics, media, and more. The school's alumni include:

- Janet Eilber, Artistic Director, Martha Graham Dance Company
- Dr. Holly Gilbert, director of the High Altitude Observatory at the National Center for Atmospheric Research
- Linda Hunt, Academy Award-winning actress
- Fred Hiebert, Archeologist-in-residence, *National Geographic*
- Jewel, Grammy Award-winning singer-songwriter
- Anthony McGill, principal clarinetist for the New York Philharmonic
- Nathaniel Mary Quinn, painter
- Doug Stanton, *New York Times* bestselling author

Graduates of Interlochen's programs have received recognition from the world's most prestigious arts accolades, including:

- 158 Grammy Awards
- 36 Tony Awards
- 27 Emmy Awards
- 14 MacArthur Fellowships

- 4 Pulitzer Prizes
- 4 Academy Awards

Many Interlochen alumni maintain deep connections to their alma mater, frequently returning to campus as guest artists, speakers, performers, and mentors to the current generation of Interlochen students. Several graduates – including *New York Times* bestselling author Dr. Brittany Cavallaro and Cristian Măcelaru, Grammy Award-winning music director of the Cincinnati Symphony Orchestra – currently serve as members of the school's faculty.

Summary

Since its founding in 1962, Interlochen Arts Academy has been a leader in both the boarding school community and the creative youth development movement. An internationally recognized destination for unparalleled artistic and academic education, Interlochen continues to empower students from around the globe to transform their passion and potential into purpose – instilling the creativity and confidence to pursue lives of significance.

Hawai'i Preparatory Academy

Location: Kamuela, Hawai'i

Year Founded: 1949

Grades Served: K–12 + Post Grad

Total Enrollment: 220 K–8, 380 9–12 + Post Grad

Percent Boarding: 40% (High School & Post Grad Only)

Percent Non-White: 60%

Percent From Out of State: 80%

Percent From Out of Country: 50%

2025–26 School Year Tuition: $71,400

Percent Who Receive Financial Aid: 45%

School Website: www.hpa.edu

Head of School: Fred Wawner

Hawai'i Preparatory Academy

Chapter Completed By

Leah Lavin, Advancement Writer

Having the opportunity to camp at Kīholo Bay and conduct scientific research on Hawaiian green sea turtles was absolutely life-changing as a teenager! It literally changed the trajectory of my future, and I am proud to say that I have now worked for NOAA for over 20 years helping to protect and conserve America's underwater treasures, which includes the important ecosystems for these endangered sea turtles.

– Claire '90

Riding horseback through the hills and adjacent tracts, the opulence of the rolling, green grassy hills and the swooping terrain up to the peak of Maunakea are etched into my mind – peace and beauty.

– Don '58

Mālama kaiāulu acknowledges that spirit, land, and people are all connected. These three things are also within each one of us, which is why caring for a place, wherever you are, is both an act of generosity and self love. As all alumni know, 'here' stays with you – it's inside you.

– Renee '98

This year in our Sustainable Food Systems class I've been able to plant and harvest food for our community, I've explored the Hawaiian Lunar calendar and how to plant with the moon phases, and I've learned elements of landscape design. Being in the garden makes me feel like I've accomplished something good, no matter what else happens in my day.

– Levi '25

A School Between Worlds

Hawaiʻi is a place of extraordinary natural beauty – coastlines carved by lava, cloud forests, dry forests, rain forests, and rainbows. But it is far more than a postcard paradise. Hawaiʻi is a complex and dynamic place that invites a deeper kind of attention: to the wonders of the natural world, to the delicate balance that sustains life, and to Hawaiian ways of knowing that have long centered care, connection, and responsibility to the land and sea. In the town of Waimea, on Hawaiʻi Island, Hawaiʻi Preparatory Academy (HPA) stands at a meeting point. It occupies both a literal and metaphorical intersection – between wet and dry, past and future, rootedness and reach.

Waimea, also known as Kamuela, lies between the green, rain-soaked hills and valleys of the windward side of the island, and the open, arid grasslands that stretch toward the sunny Kona coast. Technicolor rainbows are frequent in this borderland, and this familiar arc of ānuenue across HPA's campus never gets old.

In this landscape of contrasts and movement, it's fitting that HPA's emblem – the element that defines those who are of the school – is Ka Makani (the wind). Ka Makani is the school's rallying cry and its identity: dynamic, ever-changing, and deeply rooted in place. Like the winds that shape the island's ecosystems, HPA students can be both gentle and fierce, moving with purpose and shaping their surroundings with intention.

HPA was founded in 1949, in the years following World War II: a time of rebuilding and reimagining. Like many independent schools born in that era, it has evolved beyond its original shape. And yet, from its earliest days, HPA has been marked by a particular tension: how to be both of this place and open to the world. That dynamic runs through every part of school life. Students learn to code and to compost, to reflect and to act, to honor tradition while imagining what comes next. They're as likely to plant seedlings for native forest restoration on a sacred mauna (mountain) as they are to enter a formal research partnership with NOAA or NASA.

The school's setting reinforces this duality. Waimea is a growing town of about 10,000, home to ranchers, astronomers, scientists, artists, and cultural practitioners. It carries two names: "Waimea," meaning "reddish water," evoking the earthy tint of mountain streams; and "Kamuela," the Hawaiian rendering of "Samuel," after Samuel Parker, whose vast ranch once defined this region. That blending of indigenous and Western histories is not just linguistic – it is also a reflection of the complex intersections students learn to navigate.

At HPA, students move between digital tools and the natural world, academic rigor and emotional intelligence, independence and interdependence. The school embraces these contrasts not as competing values, but as necessary partners. The work of education here is not to resolve tension, but to live within it – to balance, stretch, listen, and grow.

This chapter tells the story of a school shaped by its surroundings and guided by a belief in possibility. HPA is a place where students are taught not to choose between worlds, but to walk thoughtfully between them.

Learning That's Rooted in Place

Learning at HPA doesn't happen apart from the land – it happens because of it. The island itself is part of the curriculum, and students are encouraged from their earliest days to understand that Hawaiʻi is not simply a place to live, but a place to care for, to study, and to listen to.

In 2019, HPA adopted the framework of Mālama Kaiāulu – a commitment to care for our community of spirit, land, and people. This framework threads through every part of the school, from renewable energy goals to relationship-building, from fifth grade garden classes to senior capstones. It shapes how students move through their day, how teachers frame their lessons, and how the school defines success – not as individual achievement alone, but as contribution to something larger.

Students learn not only the scientific names of native plants, but their uses and histories. In two campus gardens, students from kindergarten through twelfth grade engage in sustainable agriculture, learning to steward soil, grow food, and respect the delicate systems that support life. They plant and tend "canoe crops," they eat the food they help to grow, and they grow enough to share with the larger Waimea community.

Place-based education at HPA is expansive, reaching far beyond the gardens alone. Students explore Hawaiian language and culture through mele and oli (songs and chants), hula and protocol, history and voyaging. In the Lower School, Hawaiian Studies are integrated into weekly rhythms; in the Upper School, they take shape in coursework and research. Along the way, students gain more than cultural literacy – they gain a sense of kuleana, or responsibility, to care for the places and communities that sustain them.

Architecture, too, reflects this ethos. Renowned mid-century architect Vladimir Ossipoff, an early champion of site sensitivity and working within limits, created the school's original buildings to sit lightly on the land. His vision – buildings that breathe, that open to wind and light – have shaped the tone and flow of HPA's campus for generations. That tradition continues in the Energy Lab, a net-zero energy facility and one of the first K–12 buildings in the world to earn the Living Building Challenge certification. In the Energy Lab, students design experiments, analyze data, and imagine more sustainable futures.

Throughout their journey, HPA students engage in long-term projects – capstones – that tie together personal passion, academic research, and real-world impact. Whether they're building prosthetics, releasing a 9-track album of original music on Spotify, or writing a provision to a tax credit to incentivize solar power, students are expected not just to learn, but to contribute.

To be rooted in place at HPA is not to stay still. It's to grow with intention, to deepen relationships, and to carry forward a sense of responsibility that extends far beyond campus. The land teaches students to pay attention – and, more importantly, to respond.

Island Wisdom, Global Purpose

To be grounded in Hawaiʻi is not to be isolated from the world. In fact, at HPA, a deep respect for place strengthens students' sense of responsibility beyond it. From their earliest days on campus, students are encouraged to see themselves as part of a complex, interconnected world – rooted locally, reaching globally.

HPA's community includes students from across the Hawaiian Islands and around the globe, with students from across the continental US and more than 20 foreign countries represented. On any given day in the dorms, you might hear Korean, Spanish, Japanese, or German. Students arrive with different worldviews, customs, and experiences – and learn to live together, eat together, study together, and build friendships that cross cultures. In that way, the residence halls are more than living spaces; they are small international communities where compassion, curiosity, and communication are daily practices.

This global diversity isn't just an incidental feature of HPA – it's part of the school's educational philosophy. In an age of disconnection and division, HPA offers a model of how young people from different backgrounds can live in community, navigate differences, and discover common purpose. The boarding and residential life program fosters independence, yes – but also cultural exchange and deep listening. Over time, students learn not just how to live with others, but how to live well with others.

Academically, HPA's curriculum invites students to think across borders – geographic, disciplinary, and cultural. Global themes are woven into every division, from climate science and food systems to literature, political studies, and entrepreneurship. Students engage in project-based learning that encourages them to look outward: What are the ripple effects of local actions? How does history shape migration and identity? What does sustainability mean on an island – and in a global economy?

At the same time, the school maintains a strong commitment to Hawaiian host culture, not as content to be "covered," but as a lens for understanding systems, relationships, and responsibility. That foundation allows HPA's global education to be rooted in values that deepen students' sense of place even as they prepare to step into the wider world. Hawaiian culture doesn't recede in the face of globalism here; it grounds and informs it.

In today's unsettled social and political climate, HPA's Pacific location offers a safe harbor. For international families seeking a U.S.-based education that honors both academic excellence and cultural depth, Hawai'i represents a compelling option. It's a place where students are challenged to grow – and given the space to do so with care.

By the time they graduate, HPA students have experienced a rare kind of education: one that honors local knowledge and global thinking, individual agency and community responsibility. They understand that wisdom can be inherited and shared, that purpose can be personal and collective. And they carry those understandings with them – wherever they go next.

The global reach of HPA today stands on a foundation laid over generations. Even as the school grows in complexity and vision, its roots in the history and culture of Waimea remain visible. HPA's identity is not fixed, but evolving – shaped by changing times, deep traditions, and a willingness to adapt with integrity. To understand the school's future, it helps to look back.

Honoring Legacy, Embracing Change

HPA was founded in 1949 to serve the children of sugar plantation workers on Hawai'i Island. In the early years, the school was modest in scale, and its original campus in Waimea was housed in former marine barracks. The decision to welcome boarders from O'ahu came early on – partly to strengthen enrollment, partly to expand opportunity. From the beginning, HPA was coeducational, and notably, several founding board members were women – uncommon for the time, but well within keeping of the school's independent spirit.

HPA's location in Waimea meant that its early culture was shaped not just by the island's "vigorous" natural climate, but by ranch life as well. The paniolo (Hawaiian cowboy) traditions of Parker Ranch – the largest privately owned cattle operation in the United States at the time and for many decades on – left a lasting imprint on the school. Today, Parker Ranch is owned by the Parker Ranch Foundation Trust, established by Richard Smart – the last direct descendant of ranch founder John Palmer Parker – as a lasting gift to Waimea. Through the Trust, Smart ensured the ranch would benefit his hometown in perpetuity by supporting four nonprofits, including HPA. To this day, HPA students and alumni wear red palaka shirts (the traditional plaid work shirt of the paniolo) with pride... and horses born and raised on campus have been an important part of school life since the 1950s. These traditions are more than nostalgic – they are expressions of respect for the people and ways of life that built this place.

Some traditions at HPA offer windows into the school's enduring spirit. The chapel program, for example, reflects a long-held commitment to reflection, shared values, and a sense of community. Though it began during the school's early years as part of its Episcopal heritage, today the program is intentionally non-denominational and inclusive – a gathering space where students and faculty explore meaning, purpose, and ethical living together. The annual HPA Olympics, launched in the 1970s, captures a different aspect of HPA's spirit: playfulness, camaraderie, and a hard core competitive spirit. And the sea turtle research program, which began in the 1980s, reveals a deep commitment to hands-on, place-based learning with real-world impact. Each of these traditions speaks to a different facet of the HPA experience – character, joy, purpose – and together they form a thread of continuity that stretches across generations.

But tradition alone doesn't define HPA. What has made the school resilient is its ability to evolve. In recent years, HPA has taken bold steps in areas like sustainability, aiming to become carbon net zero by 2030 and embedding environmental stewardship throughout its curriculum and operations. The school has also made intentional investments in a culture of belonging – expanding its faculty training, updating curriculum, and reexamining policies to create a more just and inclusive community. Technology, too, has been integrated in thoughtful ways, from digital storytelling to a student-built, solar-powered AI model.

These changes are not surface-level. They reflect a school that is preparing its students not just to succeed in the world as it is, but to help shape the world as it could be. HPA students learn how to hold complexity, how to honor the past without being bound by it, and how to imagine futures rooted in justice, ingenuity, and care. There is no question that the school's greatest contributions to the world are Ka Makani alumni: individuals of exceptional heart and character.

Willing to Grow

Hawaiʻi Preparatory Academy stands as a testament to what education can be when it is rooted in place, guided by purpose, and open to change. From its earliest days, HPA has embodied the dualities of its setting – between mountain and sea, rain and sun, history and innovation. Rather than shy away from these contrasts, the school embraces them as essential to its identity. It is in this dynamic tension that HPA finds its strength.

To attend HPA is to step into a community that understands learning as both a personal and collective endeavor. Students are challenged to think critically, act ethically, and contribute meaningfully – not in abstraction, but in context. They study complex systems by engaging with them directly: restoring native forests, tracking sea turtles, building solar-powered technologies, or navigating relationships across cultures. The work is real, relevant, and often unfinished – and that's by design. At HPA, education is not about reaching an endpoint; it is about learning to live in relationship with others, with the land, and with the unknown.

That relationship begins with the land itself. Hawai'i Island is a powerful teacher, and HPA's curriculum honors that truth. From kindergarten to senior year, students learn that knowledge is not confined to classrooms – it also resides in soil, tide pools, wind patterns, and ancestral practices. The framework of Mālama Kaiāulu – caring for the spirit, land, and people of our community – is more than a slogan. It is a lived value, expressed in choices both large and small: how students care for campus gardens, how teachers design their lessons, how the school sets goals for sustainability and belonging. At every level, HPA asks its students to consider not just what they know, but what they will do with that knowledge – and who they are becoming in the process.

Equally important is the school's commitment to preparing students for a global future. HPA's student body reflects a remarkable diversity of cultures, languages, and perspectives, and the school sees this diversity as a gift. It challenges students to listen deeply, communicate across differences, and form relationships built on respect. In the residence halls, in the classroom, and out in the world, students practice the skills of global citizenship – grounded in a clear understanding of who they are and where they come from.

The journey from HPA to college is not a sudden leap, but an unfolding – shaped by years of real-world learning, close mentoring, and intentional reflection. A senior researching climate resilience on campus may find themselves drawn to environmental science programs across the country. A boarding student from Italy whose senior capstone focused on cross-cultural dialogue might discover a passion for international relations.

A junior who builds a robot to clean solar panels in the Energy Lab could land in an engineering cohort at a top university, having already experienced the rigors of iterative design and public presentation. At every stage, students are encouraged to ask not just where they want to go next, but why – and to develop the voice and clarity to answer that question with purpose.

Coming from one of the most geographically remote and demographically underrepresented states, HPA students offer colleges a rare combination: global awareness shaped by local grounding, and academic excellence shaped by lived experience. Students carry with them the perspective of island life, of learning in relationship with land and culture, of seeing the world not just through screens or textbooks, but through tide pools, telescopes, and traditions. In a national admissions landscape that values authentic experience and original thinking, HPA students bring both – and they bring them from a place few others can claim. It's not uncommon to see HPA seniors admitted to a wide range of selective colleges and universities – not just for their transcripts, but for the depth of perspective and curiosity they carry with them.

As HPA looks to the future, it carries forward a deep respect for the traditions that have shaped it: the independent spirit of its founders, the resilience of Waimea's ranching community, the wisdom of Hawaiian culture, and the curiosity of generations of students who have dared to ask hard questions. But tradition alone does not define the school. What defines HPA is its willingness to grow – to evolve its practices, examine its impact, and prepare young people to face an uncertain future with courage, creativity, and care.

HPA's graduates are thinkers and doers, caretakers and change makers – grounded, like the school itself, in a place between worlds.

Midland School

Location: Los Olivos, California

Year Founded: 1932

Grades Served: 9–12

Total Enrollment: 85

Percent Boarding: 100%

Percent Non-White: 49%

Percent From Out of State: 14%

Percent From Out of Country: 18%

2025–26 School Year Tuition: $81,900

Percent Who Receive Financial Aid: 55%

School Website: www.midland-school.org

Head of School: Hannah Nelson

Midland School

Submission Completed By

Shona McCarthy, Andrew McCarthy '85, Hannah Nelson, Cierra Rickman, Ellie Moore, Dan Susman

My headlamp shines a dim spotlight onto the center of a small circle of girls. We sit around a Whisperlite backpacking stove, watching like hungry hawks as I place a thinly-sliced-and-perfectly-spiced potato into the pot of hot oil.

Almost every weekend, five to ten friends and I spend our Friday night hiking a few miles from our dorms on a student-led camping trip, a simple yet ample way to enjoy the rolling grasslands that whisper in the wind and the ancient-burly oaks that have borne witness to generations of students just like me.

For the last 2 years, this has been my idea of a weekend night well spent, an overnight representation of the sweat on our backs as we sowed seeds and weeded the ground to grow that now-crispy potato on our school's farm. Of the 16-hour Wilderness First-Aid course and days spent learning risk management and outdoor leadership in order to gain the trust from faculty to take my peers on overnight camping trips. Of the senior who two years ago thought to invite a timid freshman (me) to join them for a night among the crickets, cozy in sleeping bags while we shared stories and laughter.

Many high schoolers spend their Friday nights at ragers or strip malls. I prefer the shooting stars over my head, the crackling warmth of a campfire, and the satisfying crunch of a freshly fried potato.

– Amelie Grant, Midland '27

A School Built by Hand

In 1932, amid the worst economic crisis in American history, Paul Squibb wrote a letter to friends announcing his intent to start a school.

There would be no kitchen staff. No janitors. No luxuries. Just students, teachers, and a stretch of wild California land. Squibb wasn't looking to start a school in the usual sense. He was building a place to teach the values of self-reliance, community, and simplicity. He called it Midland. The first seven students lived in the Main House with the faculty. They chopped wood for heat, hauled water by hand, constructed board and batten classrooms and cabins, and built timber desks to sit solid on a gravel floor.

The idea of the place was not to escape the real world but to learn how to live within it, with purpose, discipline, and care. "Our school will be operated on the self-help plan," he wrote. "Which means every boy will be obliged in part to work his way through."

Nearly a century later, the founding beliefs still hold: that young people are not only capable of meaningful work, but that such work is essential to their growth. That character, not comfort, is the foundation of a life well lived. Born in the wake of the Great Depression, Midland's financial assistance philosophy also remains firmly in place, set in the principle that no student should be turned away based on the ability to pay.

A Midland education began with a student, a teacher, and an idea. Today, the school carries that essential spirit, developing academic excellence alongside life skills that matter: curiosity, communication, critical thinking, and the confidence to lead.

A Place of Purpose

Midland sits on 2,860 acres, rising to the edge of the Los Padres National Forest. Oak woodland, chaparral, serpentine ridges, and sagebrush adorn this slice of California's Santa Ynez Valley, an ancestral Chumash landscape. Honoring people who stewarded this land long before Midland is foundational to students' emerging connection to place. Whether they are studying the geology and ecology of the land itself, the Chumash ethnobotanical uses of local plants, discussing cultural amalgamation and "double consciousness" through the lens of Leslie Marmon Silko's novel, "Ceremony," or unpacking the history of European settlers and tribal sovereignty in U.S. History, Midland students dig into a myriad of histories and cultures with depth and nuance.

The school's campus has three main areas: student cabins are in Upper Yard and Lower Yard, while Middle Yard is the academic and communal center. Students share a cabin with a roommate and the occasional pet. Faculty homes are interspersed throughout.

> *Eight classrooms, two barns, ten acres of farm, and twenty-three cabins – I can see all of these buildings laid out like dollhouses as I sit perched on a cliff edge five hundred feet*

above Middle Yard, where most of the student body sits in classes.

– Jay Liu, Midland '27

Place shapes Midland's pedagogy. Students learn to see this landscape as a layered story, where new ideas and experiences are added to what came before. Science students track the watershed to measure changes after rain. In History, they apply knowledge of the Columbian exchange as they examine the historical roots of the cultivated and native plants found on the property. Art explorations draw from the surroundings, crafting insects from natural materials and honing surfboards from salvaged wood. One day each year, students wake to the news that classes have been cancelled. Everyone, as a group, hikes together to the 3,685' peak of *Owotoponus*, or Grass Mountain, overlooking the campus all the way to the Pacific Ocean.

The lights are off – it's well past curfew. Curled in a ball around my roommate's snoring white Labrador Retriever, I stuff my face into my pillow as my body shakes with laughter... Whispers of teenage gossip, a homework assignment breakdown, an idea brain-dump session, or a late-night deep dive into the intricacies of growing up in such a complex world.

As I drift into sleep, I know that whatever happens, I will always fit here: letting my body rest after a day of learning, challenging myself, and working alongside my peers to make this place a little better than before, whispering 'goodnight, I love you' to the girl who lays across the room from me, a stranger-turned-sister from these two years living together at Midland.

– Amelie Grant, Midland '27

Right Where You Want To Be

Midland is intentionally scaled: eighty-some students, thirtyish faculty and staff. All students live on campus. Faculty do, too. What results is not just familiarity, but *shared lives* – meals, conversation, collaboration, and interconnected learning.

Midland days begin with work. Students clean classrooms, tend horses, harvest vegetables, or split kindling. Breakfast is in Stillman Hall, followed by classes and a student-grown midday meal. Twice-daily, Assembly includes announcements, celebration, or recruitment for an upcoming event or need.

Afternoon activities shift with the season: mountain biking, outdoor leadership, horsemanship, trailwork, cross-country, soccer, or time on the farm. Family-style dinner, students settle into study hall, then a final social 'tea time' for a snack before bed. Evenings end with Prefect check-ins and final faculty rounds.

Tuesday and Thursday afternoons are unstructured free time known as Half Holidays. Weekends include learning through real work experience, student-led overnight trips, time for study, and rest. After a Sunday morning sleep-in, students join faculty for the week's formal Work Period to maintain and care for their campus home.

Before coming to Midland, all of my schools looked the same: hallways, lockers, paved playgrounds, and few trees. Midland is the complete opposite. We live in cabins on a ranch surrounded by open sky, oak trees, and mountains. I wake up to the sound of birds or sometimes chickens, and I walk past horses throughout my day.

There's so much nature here, it's wild. We hike, backpack, ride horses, and spend weekends doing "hardluck hikes" that push us out of our comfort zones. It's tough, but also kind of amazing. You end up learning a lot about yourself out there. Midland challenges you in the best way.

– Pyp Pratt, Midland '27

The academic year unfolds across a series of six-week terms, each followed by a break without assigned homework; focused work during term time and full rest in between.

Back in the 1940s, when Squibb noticed students returned from fall break sick and depleted, he began inviting parents, grandparents, siblings, alumni, and friends to campus for Thanksgiving. Each year, around 500 people gather at Midland for a bountiful community meal.

MIDterms, held twice each year, are week-long, fully immersive experiential learning opportunities for hands-on student projects and ideas that don't fit neatly into the regular schedule. Everything from groups exploring food security at urban farms in Los Angeles to researching and writing a play that explored Midland's past, present, and future.

Monday and Thursday evenings include an all-school gathering in the chapel, a secular space for talks exploring the community experience – personal stories, hard-won insight, forward-dreaming, and scholarship.

Chapel, an ancient wooden building as old as the school – approaching a hundred years of use. Originally a milking parlor, it is the most reverent place on campus. The walls are covered by ninety-three wooden boards, each containing the hand-painted names of every student who has ever completed a year at Midland.

Some days, the silence is only broken by someone delivering life lessons a local from their hometown taught them. On others, stifled tears as a teary-eyed faculty grieves a lost family member, or shares the wisdom their passed grandmother granted them. And some days the walls ring with laughter, as someone shares the funniest stories they have kept secret since freshman year. But what remains constant is the insight imparted and the community created.

– Jay Liu, Midland '27

Students Take Ownership of Their Education

Midland's academic program is grounded in real-world application. Students meet University of California A–G requirements. Graduates regularly move on to exceptional colleges and universities, as well as extraordinary programs in horsemanship, outdoor leadership, and agriculture.

Students are guided in seven core competencies: critical thinking and analysis, craftsmanship, problem solving, literacy and voice, being of use, connection to place and environment, and commitment to diversity, equity, inclusion, and justice. Students receive direct feedback. They revise. They retake. They grow. Skills are practiced everywhere: on paper, in dialogue, in the lab, at the woodpile, on horseback, in the strawberry rows, and on the trail.

Technology is a tool here, not the center of campus life. Students hand over their phones at the beginning of each term. The Internet and AI are here as academic resources; learning and community do not rely on them. In the absence of constant distraction, conversations stretch, friendships deepen, mountain bikes find trails, music emerges, and time is no longer split into tabs.

Students progress to take ownership of their education. Each senior completes and presents a self-directed capstone thesis or project: independent studies rooted in questions and problems they care about. They conduct comparative studies of U.S. History curricula across America to understand political polarization; they build mountain biking trails and surfcrafts for their fellow Midlanders; and they apply coding skills to create a video game based on their school.

With mastery comes opportunity for leadership – through teaching and mentoring younger students and taking on real responsibility within the community. Students lead job crews, manage gear rooms, guide outdoor trips, mediate peer dynamics, and run assemblies.

Students also organize groups and events that share their cultures, histories, and traditions with the broader community, expanding understanding through lived experience rather than abstraction.

At Midland, the work of supporting and considering diversity, equity, inclusion and justice isn't siloed into a single class or a handful of dates on the calendar. It is alive in the fabric of each day, from equitable grading policies to monthly film festivals and workshops and a restorative accountability system, grounded in clear expectations and shared responsibility. Courses are designed to present students with both "mirrors" of their own experience and "windows" into perspectives and identities distinct from their own.

> *I wander through Stillman – our dining hall transformed into a gallery for our Diversity, Equity, Inclusion and Justice Summit. Everyone is here exploring so many artifacts of learning. I see student's takeaways from workshops about*

color symbolism in traditional Chinese culture, Black resilience and resistance through hip hop, ableism and activism in the modern age, and the disproportionate impacts of climate change on marginalized communities. I stand in awe of these young people who have opted to spend their free time over lunches and afternoons over the past six weeks planning workshops and film discussions about topics close to their identities – and their peers who engage with genuine curiosity and respect. I think of our Asian American Alliance working closely with the extraordinary staff who make Midland's food to cook an elaborate multi-course meal for one hundred of us to celebrate Lunar New Year. And "Queercus" (LGBTQIA+ group) putting on a Drag Show that brought us together in joyful celebration. I remember LatinX bringing Dia de los Muertos *to life: an incredible* ofrenda *of farm-grown marigolds, papel picado banners and painted* calaveras *to honor our loved ones who have crossed over. Ours is a community small enough for everyone to be known, to have a real voice and impact, and where belonging is a co-creation that makes the whole greater than the sum of its parts.*

– Ellie Moore, Associate Head of School

Jobs, Leadership, Growth and Responsibility

Students rotate through daily jobs that keep the campus running. With experience, they take on more responsibility – leading crews, mentoring peers, managing gear rooms, and serving as prefects. The Student Council works with faculty and the Head of School to adjudicate major rule infractions. These roles demand initiative, communication, and leadership skills that many young people don't encounter until college or beyond. Students are held both capable of and accountable for delivering on their responsibilities. Through every facet of autonomy and interdependence, students are supported to learn as their best selves.

> *At Midland, helping out is just part of life. Students clean bathrooms, wash dishes, and muck out stalls. Jobs I'd never done before. I didn't even do my laundry at home. Our prefects check our work and help us stay on track. They're not harsh, but they do expect us to take our jobs seriously.*
>
> – Pyp Pratt, Midland '27

Accountability to self and to community is foundational to a Midland education. A job left undone or a choice to break school rules often has an impact on others. Consequences for those actions are considered opportunities for both repair and learning. Midland's 'lap system' is simple and consistent, requiring students to spend a designated portion of their free time on community work in restoration of their mistake.

Horses, Farming, and Meaningful Work at the Edge of Wilderness

Some of the most remarkable moments at Midland start with a shovel, a pack, a saddle, a saw, or a seed.

Outdoor Leadership takes students into the extended campus. Trips range from nearby swimming holes to high-country mountaineering routes. Others cross into the Los Padres National Forest for days (and occasionally weeks) at a time. Students lead trips, cook meals, navigate trails, and manage safety. By senior year, many are teaching these skills, and spearheading student-only overnights on the property, called Hardlucks, one of the most beloved Midland traditions.

Before becoming a Midlander, I had never touched a horse, let alone ridden one. Midland attracted me through the prospect of backpacking and hiking around the large property with hills and cliffs – I never even pictured riding on horseback. But after a year here, I knew I had to branch out and sample everything the school had to offer.

– Jay Liu, Midland '27

Horses give students a chance to practice husbandry and self-awareness through riding, training, and tending to their four-legged partners. Riders learn natural horsemanship, starting with groundwork and trail basics. Often riders expand their skills into cattle work, gaining exposure to real ranch horsemanship and stock sense. Midland's twenty-horse herd lives on campus year-round and is cared for every day by students, creating deep familiarity and genuine partnership. With more than twenty-five miles of riding trails winding through oak groves, a large arena, and a fully equipped tack room, students gain firsthand experience not just in riding, but in stewardship, communication, and patience.

The food students grow at Midland makes up more than half what the community eats: pickled beets in the salad bar, roasted squash with campus-raised pork, strawberries turned into ice cream by student hands. The school's 10-acre organic farm and garden brings routine – digging, weeding, harvesting – and also delight. Students wash carrots, haul compost, and learn when a melon is ready by how it smells. They slip out to the rows between classes for ripe strawberries. The farm teaches students to notice, contribute, and take pride in feeding people.

> *The people here are just as unique as the landscape. Everyone comes from different backgrounds. Some students wear flannel shirts and boots; others wear graphic tees and beanies. There's freedom to be yourself, but that comes with responsibility.*
>
> – Pyp Pratt Midland '27

Trail building gives students a lasting way to shape the place. They cut switchbacks, lay drainage, and reroute erosion-prone paths. Mountain biking, the most recent addition to Midland's experiential curriculum, emerged from this work. Students ride the trails they've built, tasting the fast and dusty fruit of their own labor. Alumni return to campus years and even decades later to hike to the trails they hand-crafted with friends and faculty. Parts of the extended campus trail system are available to the public through a conservation agreement with the county.

For the Curious, the Adventurous, and Those Who Wish to Be

> *Today we are seeing the dreams of inspired poets merging with the findings of careful scientists. The dreamer and the doer are showing the thinker new vistas of life on earth. New glories are coming to light for thoughtful minds.*
>
> – Paul Squibb, Founder, 1932

The people who choose Midland are curious thinkers and active learners, often with strong academic records, looking for a school that feels more connected, more hands-on, more whole. Students come from cities, rural towns, far away countries, public schools, and homeschooling. The admissions team says they can see immediately when a visiting student knows Midland is *right where they want to be.*

Midlanders care about how things are made, where things come from, and whom they affect. They seek academic challenge and dialogue within disagreement. They ask big questions and are willing to live inside them. They are looking for belonging, and they are willing to help build it.

Faculty arrive with similar instincts. They come to teach what matters and to live in rhythm with the values they hold. Many hold advanced degrees in their disciplines. All are deeply invested in the practice of teaching through lived experience and find purpose in helping students develop core skills and competencies. Midland faculty advise, mentor, lead trips, and are fully embedded in school life.

> *English class on Thursday morning carries the joyful echo of surfing together on Wednesday afternoon. At dinner, we eat food that we grew and harvested here with our own hands. Learning, exploring, growing, and living together strengthens our relationships, and becomes the fabric of this place. Here, time feels thicker, slower, more nutritious and complete.*
>
> – John Babbott, Humanities Faculty

The Beginning of a Lifelong Path

Midland graduates leave for competitive colleges and careers, but most importantly prepared for lives with purpose and direction. Graduates carry with them other things, too: a bias toward usefulness; an instinct to contribute before they critique; and an unshakable understanding of what it means to belong to place, to community, and to themselves.

> *I can trace so many threads back to those four years in the Santa Ynez Valley. I learned the contours of Midland's*

> *landscape and the names of native species. I learned to troubleshoot a solar panel malfunction, to manage a team of peers while running the dish crew, and to stay calm when a horse spooked on the trail. I discovered how to advocate for myself professionally and lead others through difficult times.*
>
> *The writing and analytical abilities I developed in Midland's English and History classes carried me through a degree in English Literature from Whitman College and a master's degree in Publishing & Writing from Emerson College.*
>
> – Emma Struebing, Midland '16

Students find at Midland a path to discovering and building the person they want to be: the artist, the mountaineer, the designer, the engineer. Midland graduates leave not just with acquired knowledge, but with a stronger sense of who they are, what it means to be of use, and to belong.

> *I don't often chop wood anymore. In my adventures after Midland – from Williams College in Massachusetts to a Masters in Physics at the University of British Columbia to managing the Climbers Ranch in Grand Teton – I've realized that wood chopping was never really the point.*
>
> *Each of these experiences underscored for me the key values that Midland teaches at the woodpile: find what you need, work in service of those around you, better yourself and the place you are in. Those values still drive me.*
>
> – Duncan McCarthy '17

Middlebridge School

Location: Narragansett, Rhode Island

Year Founded: 2008

Grades Served: 9–12 + Post Grad

Total Enrollment: 80

Percent Boarding: 95%

Percent Non-White: 22%

Percent From Out of State: 92%

Percent From Out of Country: 10%

2025–26 School Year Tuition: $106,950

Percent Who Receive Financial Aid: 21%

School Website: www.middlebridgeschool.org

Head of School: John J. Kaufman

Middlebridge School

Chapter Completed By

John J. Kaufman, Head of School

Middlebridge School's Motto: *A Community Where Difference is Celebrated, Potential is Cultivated, and Belonging and Transformation.*

Nestled on a scenic oceanfront campus in Narragansett, Rhode Island, Middlebridge School is a coeducational boarding and day high school intentionally designed for students with learning differences.

Steps from the shoreline and within reach of miles of beaches and destinations such as Newport, Mystic Seaport, and Block Island, our campus evokes a coastal culture that encourages students and families to breathe deeply, appreciate the ocean air, and explore everything a seaside town has to offer, from local ice cream parlors to fresh Narragansett Bay seafood.

Tucked back from Ocean Road, Hazard Castle, a historic neo-Gothic structure built in the 1800s, has served as Middlebridge's home since 2012. Our location fuels signature programming in environmental, marine, and agricultural sciences, adventure learning, and artistic inspiration.

In practice, a signature independent study project in our Environmental Science program saw a sophomore student apply for permits with the Department of Fish and Wildlife to rewild our campus freshwater pond with four breeds of local fish. Proximity to the ocean provides opportunities for experiential learning, environmental stewardship, and outdoor education. Whether it's kayaking on the bay, studying tidal ecosystems, or taking in the calming effect of the sea, our coastal setting fosters academic engagement and emotional well-being.

Founded in 2008 with 18 students and a handful of passionate educators, Middlebridge began as a scrappy startup with a bold vision: to reimagine education for bright students who learn differently. With limited resources but unwavering commitment, the founding team built a school, from the ground up, rooted in connection, creativity, and student-centered support. Our first accreditation report from the New England Association of Schools and Colleges (NEASC) described the faculty's commitment with the phrase "missionary zeal." From those humble beginnings, Middlebridge has grown into a nationally recognized boarding school while retaining the entrepreneurial spirit and individualized care that defined its earliest days.

We are often compared to schools with decades or even centuries of history. Our "startup spirit" means centuries-old traditions don't bind Middlebridge – we get to build our own. This freedom allows the community to be intentional and responsive, crafting programs and traditions that reflect the needs and strengths of our students today. From signature events to student-led initiatives, everything at Middlebridge is designed with purpose, not just legacy.

At Middlebridge, learning differences are seen as an invitation to teach and gain knowledge differently. We reimagine academic success, cultivating a culture where students are known deeply, taught intentionally, and empowered to thrive authentically.

To be named among the 16 Elevated Boarding Schools in America is an honor – and a testament to the community ethos and mission that have defined Middlebridge since its founding in 2008. We are not simply a conventional college-preparatory school that adds accommodations. We are a purpose-built learning environment that centers the strengths and needs of neurodivergent learners, building academic confidence and social-emotional resilience within a warm, vibrant, and student-centered culture. This is the story of Middlebridge School: who we are, what we do differently, and why it works.

Our Founding Philosophy: Whole Student, Whole Community

Middlebridge was founded with a clear mission: to serve students with learning differences such as dyslexia, dysgraphia, ADHD, executive functioning challenges, and other language-based learning needs. But our vision went beyond remediation or academic support; it was about building a school where students who often feel marginalized in traditional settings could thrive academically, socially, and emotionally.

Serving marginalized students means more than offering academic coaching; it involves recognizing the whole student. With 75–80 students and 75 faculty members in our community, we notice when a student misses breakfast, skips basketball practice, or is late with their math homework. "Seeing" our students means knowing when we can encourage them to show up as their whole and authentic selves: lead younger students, sign up for an internship at the University of Rhode Island, or audition for the lead in the school play. We can foster genuine leadership and confidence because we come to know each enrolled student as an individual, inside and outside the classroom.

When students feel genuinely known and seen in high school, it can transform their sense of possibility. At Middlebridge, strong relationships with faculty and peers help students build confidence, take risks, and pursue opportunities they might have once thought were out of reach. Being known creates a safe space for growth, where students are empowered to stretch beyond their comfort zones and discover what they're truly capable of. Real progress happens when students feel safe, understood, and empowered to be themselves.

Our founding ethos remains: when students are met with curiosity, respect, and support, they become their fullest selves.

Small by Design, Big in Impact

With a total enrollment of approximately 75–80 students and a student-to-faculty ratio of almost 1:1, Middlebridge is small by design. This allows for individualized instruction, close mentoring relationships, and a deeply collaborative community.

Our average academic class size is eight students, and students are placed in classrooms with peers who share their learning profile. Being in a small classroom with peers who share a similar learning profile can be incredibly validating and empowering. At Middlebridge, this intentional grouping allows students to learn at a pace and in a style that works for them, without fear of being misunderstood or left behind. It fosters a sense of belonging, reduces anxiety, and opens the door to deeper engagement and collaboration. As our students grow in academic confidence and skill, they are eligible to take college classes for credit at local organizations. Beyond the AP system, Middlebridge juniors and seniors generalize their academic skills in college classrooms on college campuses.

As graduate Julia, Class of '25, shares, "I have discovered the complete joy of being very vulnerably seen in a small and understanding community and classes." That sense of safety and visibility is not incidental – it's built into every layer of the Middlebridge experience.

In large public schools or hyper-competitive private schools across the country, students with learning differences often feel overlooked or overwhelmed. These environments prioritize speed, conformity, and performance over individualized support, leaving neurodivergent learners struggling to keep up or fading into the background. At Middlebridge, the focus shifts to understanding each student's unique strengths and needs, ensuring they are supported and set up to thrive.

Here, students do not get lost. Personalized learning profiles, created upon enrollment and shared with every faculty member, guide every aspect of the student's experience, from academic instruction to student life to extracurricular and internship participation. Our team approach ensures that our students' growth is supported holistically.

A Relational Approach to Learning

At Middlebridge, we emphasize a strengths-based, student-centered model that honors different cognitive styles and processing speeds. We allow for multiple modes of engagement, expression, and representation.

Students participate in rich academic programming that includes English, math, science, history, enrichment electives, and internships – but with innovative scaffolds and intentional pacing. In many classrooms, direct instruction is paired with project-based learning, experiential opportunities, and Socratic dialogue, helping students access higher-order thinking skills while remaining grounded in supportive structure.

> *You can tell that everyone here absolutely loves to teach and help. The teachers take the time to get to really know you and build a relationship with you that feels genuinely authentic and not forced. The structure here helps to build routines and set you up for success in whatever life throws at you next.*
>
> – Ruthie, Class of '24

We do not believe in one-size-fits-all education. Instead, our teachers and academic coaches work collaboratively to differentiate instruction, providing accommodations and strategies that help each learner find academic confidence.

Academic Coaching: The Heart of Executive Function Development

Executive functioning is central to many of our students' needs, and academic coaching is one of the defining pillars of a Middlebridge education. Each student meets daily, 1:1 or in pairs, with their tutor and academic coach, who serves as an executive functioning mentor, accountability partner, and study skills guide.

Coaching sessions are personalized and dynamic. A student might work on breaking down an essay into manageable steps, developing a study schedule for an upcoming exam, or practicing mindfulness before a busy day. These 1:1 sessions create space for students to reflect on academic goals, learn how to plan and prioritize, and build metacognitive awareness. At Middlebridge, we are actively working with our students to learn how they learn, know what strategies they need to succeed academically, and own their advocacy to ask for the support they may need in the future at college and in the world of work.

1:1 coaching is transformative for students with learning differences because it creates a space where they don't have to mask or hide who they are as learners. Instead of working to keep up appearances, they can focus on real growth through honest, daily relationships built on trust and understanding. This consistent, individualized support not only strengthens academic skills but also fosters resilience, self-awareness, and a healthier relationship with vulnerability.

Part of what makes our tutorial model essential is its consistency and integration. Tutors and executive function coaches attend faculty meetings, communicate with classroom teachers, and partner with student life faculty, ensuring that students are supported in how they learn across all environments.

Years after students graduate from Middlebridge, the relationship they had with their tutor can be what drives them to comfortably seek support from a professor, mentor, or colleague as they reach new milestones in life. The memory of that relationship can also be motivating. As alum Jack S. shared, "Years after graduation, when I'm calling it in on an assignment and not doing my best, it's my tutor's voice that I can hear, telling me I'm capable of doing better."

The Middlebridge Difference: A Foundation, Not Just a Feature

In 2023, Middlebridge opened our Performing Arts and Emotional Intelligence Center, a physical and philosophical hub for our campus's ongoing work around leadership, emotional intelligence, and expressive growth.

Emotional Intelligence (EI) is not an enhancement to the curriculum; it is a core part of it. Through structured lessons, candid conversations, and everyday practice, students learn to discuss their emotions, navigate challenges, and build stronger relationships.

At the heart of this initiative is our belief that Emotional Intelligence (EI) is not just a soft skill, but "the study of the self and the world around you." For adolescents amid profound emotional and social development, this work is essential. At Middlebridge, students examine how their choices, values, media consumption, and relationships shape their understanding of the world. They ask questions about identity, influence, and integrity – both in formal lessons and in the informal moments that shape real learning.

Imagine a school campus where students investigate values-based social media usage. What do their algorithms say about who they are as people? What do their friends think of the way they interact with the world on social media platforms? What about the media they consume? What language is the world giving them about how to have a healthy relationship? How is that performed and modeled for them, and what can they take away, to keep or to practice, from those stories? The value of hosting these open discussions in classrooms and on campus, for all students, is immeasurable. Our Emotional Intelligence program is one of the signature programs that every student, in every high school in the country, could benefit from.

This focus on Emotional Intelligence helps students do more than feel better – it helps them perform better. They build resilience, communicate more effectively, manage conflict with maturity, and develop a deeper sense of empathy. These aren't just useful traits; they're the foundation for healthy adulthood.

EI is embedded across campus life, integrated into our academics, student support, and community culture. Our students leave with more than academic preparation; they depart with the insight and skills to thrive in college, in relationships, and in themselves.

Traditions That Build Belonging

At heart, Middlebridge is a community built on traditions, core to the culture, that cultivate joy, connection, and shared identity. Some of our most beloved include:

- **Fall Festival, Spring Palooza, Casino Night:** Campus-wide celebrations all about fun, connection, and tradition. Whether students carve pumpkins, dress up for a night of card games and mocktails, or get their faces painted in the gentle spring light, these moments are designed to bring everyone together – no phones, just friends. These events remind us that shared experiences are just as important as academics in building a strong community.

- **Thanksgiving Gratitude Dinner:** The annual Thanksgiving Dinner at Middlebridge School is one of the most meaningful nights of the year. Gathered around a beautifully set table with faculty and peers, students stand up to share what they're grateful for in front of the community. It's a night filled with deep connection and the kind of vulnerability that builds trust and belonging.
- **Community Morning Meetings:** Every week at Middlebridge, we host a community meeting with all students and faculty to build inclusive culture. From the informal shoutout to formal recognition of a good deed or innovative independent study, we validate student efforts, build self-esteem, and foster a sense of belonging. This acknowledgment helps reinforce student identity, encourages responsibility, and supports emotional well-being during a time when connection and acceptance are especially important.

Arts, Athletics, and the "Third Space"

We believe in the transformative power of the "third space," programs and pursuits outside the classroom and dorm where students can discover passions, form friendships, and develop confidence.

Our **Arts Programming** is diverse, including theater, visual arts, digital design, music, creative writing, and yearbook, among other opportunities. Our small school has earned national recognition from Herff-Jones for two award-winning yearbooks, each driven by student creativity and voice. One edition, themed "Nestflix," playfully combined Netflix-style programming with our owl mascot, while another drew inspiration from People magazine, turning the spotlight on student personalities and community life. These publications showcase technical skills and the imagination, humor, and pride students demonstrate when given full creative ownership.

Athletics at Middlebridge is inclusive and adaptive, a no-cut program that includes gifted athletes and first-time players. The result is a culture where seasoned athletes and first-time players share the field with equal enthusiasm. We offer competitive team sports such as basketball, soccer, and golf, alongside recreational and wellness-focused options like yoga, strength training, surfing, hiking, and biking. The goal isn't just physical development, but also community, persistence, and wellness. One of the strong indicators of our athletic culture is that every team ends with more players than the season started with, as players encourage new students to join the team experience.

Our **Outdoor Exploration** program brings learning to the natural world, using challenge and adventure as vehicles for growth. Students climb rock walls, navigate ropes courses, ski and snowboard, paddleboard, and hike throughout New England. These experiences build leadership, risk tolerance, communication, and a deepened sense of trust in self and others.

> *Outside the classroom, I discovered so many new things I never knew I enjoyed. First and foremost, I fell in love with the game of golf, which has become a focal point of my life, and the three times that I had the privilege to play at Fishers Island were some of the best days of my entire Middlebridge tenure.*
>
> – Nate G., Class of '25

Together, these "third space" opportunities often serve as the spark for confidence, leadership, and the joyful self-discovery that defines the Middlebridge experience.

Purpose In Practice: Success Beyond Middlebridge

Internships at Middlebridge are a vital bridge between classroom learning and real-world experience. Through our Internship program, students engage in meaningful placements with local businesses, nonprofits, and universities, where they apply academic skills, develop professional habits, and explore future interests. Whether assisting in marine research, working in design studios, or contributing to community outreach programs, our students leave with tangible achievements and a clearer sense of their goals. Internships at Middlebridge aren't just resume builders, they are transformative opportunities that help students build confidence and responsibility, envision their future, and step into it with purpose.

In addition to real world experience and strong resumes, each student works with a transition counselor who helps them develop a post-graduation plan, write personal statements, build resumes, and navigate applications.

Our alumni attend institutions such as Villanova, University of Illinois, Lynn, Elon, New York University, and the University of Denver, among others. But just as important as where they go is who they are when they leave: confident, connected, and capable.

As a recent graduate, Riya, Class of '25, states, "Thanks to Middlebridge's support, I'll be attending one of the top acting colleges in the world."

Student Life: Learning Beyond the Classroom

As a boarding school, Middlebridge provides a learning environment where growth doesn't stop when the school day ends. Our student life program is intentional, nurturing, and integral to the student experience.

Each dorm is led by a dedicated team of student life faculty, who serve as mentors, advocates, and caregivers. Evening routines are structured to support executive functioning: there's extra time for homework, check-ins, and leisure. Weekends include group outings, community service, cultural events, and downtime for relaxation and connection.

Perhaps most importantly, student life at Middlebridge teaches independence. Students model daily living skills, navigate roommate dynamics, and learn how to advocate for themselves in real-time, real-world contexts.

Unlike many traditional schools, part of the beauty of Middlebridge student life is that students are required to engage in the community. A student might choose to cook in the kitchen, have an off-campus job or internship, join a sports team, or take a guitar lesson, but they must participate in the student life community.

Professional Development and Faculty Culture

Our faculty are not only teachers. They are leaders, researchers, mentors, artists, coaches, and caregivers. And they are committed to continual learning. Middlebridge invests heavily in professional development, with ongoing training in Orton-Gillingham literacy methods, assistive technology, creating an effective language-based classroom, digital literacy and citizenship, executive functioning coaching, trauma-informed practices, and DEIB (diversity, equity, inclusion, and belonging) frameworks.

Faculty meet daily for cross-departmental collaboration and participate in annual retreats, summer institutes, and outside conferences. The result is a highly reflective, relational, and mission-driven faculty culture.

Family Engagement and Partnership

We believe that families are our partners in student success. From the beginning of the admissions process through graduation, we cultivate open, collaborative relationships with families.

Parents and guardians receive weekly academic and residential updates, attend virtual conferences, and participate in Family Weekends filled with programming, performances, and parent workshops. Our Parent Association also offers opportunities for engagement and advocacy.

We know that many families arrive at Middlebridge after difficult educational journeys. We honor their trust and seek to rebuild a sense of hope and possibility.

> *As a parent of a recently graduated senior, my child agrees with me that the teachers were amazing, the school culture safe, growth-oriented, and positive and the overall experience tremendous. At graduation, students expressed thanks to the faculty because faculty get to know the child and are able to individualize teaching to the needs and strengths of students. Students share that they found a place to belong, created close friendships and became excited about learning after not having that experience previously. I am forever grateful that this school came into our lives and I believe the experience made the difference of a lifetime.*
>
> – Parent, Class of '24

Putting It All Together: The Middlebridge Experience

From the moment a student arrives, they're met with personal assessment, academic planning, tutoring, emotional-intelligence curriculum, real-world experience, and residential mentorship, all coordinated in an intentionally small, caring community. This integrated framework ensures individualized growth and a sense of belonging. Students thrive as they work through academic challenges in a supportive one-on-one model, learn resilience and self-awareness through EI programming, engage with the broader world via internships and college credits, and live in a community that nurtures leadership, connection, and self-reliance.

Accreditation, Outcomes, and Elevation

Middlebridge is fully accredited by NEASC and the Rhode Island Department of Education and approved by SEVP for international students. NEASC commended the community for its comprehensive programming and faculty collegiality.

To be "elevated" means to be intentional, inclusive, and inspired. Middlebridge is purpose-built for students with learning differences, not as an afterthought, but as the core of our mission. With small classes, daily coaching, an emotionally intelligent community, internships, and a campus that inspires curiosity, students don't just succeed here. They become who they're meant to be.

Middlebridge is not a traditional school with accommodations. It is intentionally structured around the strengths and needs of its learners. Every aspect of the school is designed to support this mission. Students graduate with a toolbox for coping, advocating, collaborating, and leading with empathy.

With full accreditation, 100% college acceptance, and a diversity of outcomes, Middlebridge delivers results tailored to individual student paths. This is not a place of last resort. It is a dynamic, vibrant community designed to help students who learn differently to lead confidently and become themselves fully.

The Woodhall School

Location: Bethlehem, Connecticut

Year Founded: 1983

Grades Served: Boys, 9–12

Total Enrollment: 45

- **Percent Boarding:** 100%
- **Percent Non-White:** 10%
- **Percent From Out of State:** 91%
- **Percent From Out of Country:** 7%

2025–26 School Year Tuition: $89,000

- **Percent Who Receive Financial Aid:** 20%

School Website: www.woodhallschool.org

Head of School: Matthew C. Woodhall

The Woodhall School

Chapter Completed By
Matthew C. Woodhall, Head of School

The Woodhall School: The Phoenix Rising

"I can't. So, I won't." "Why try? I'll only fail." Or "Why try? I won't know what to do if I succeed." These words whether said, thought, or felt reflect the mindset of many of the boys before they begin their journey at The Woodhall School.

Set on forty woodland acres in the Litchfield Hills of Connecticut, Woodhall provides opportunities for success for a particular kind of bright, neurodiverse boy who may defy easy categorization. Yet, each boy presents with a fragile self-esteem, having experienced a paradoxical divide between potential and performance and between his desire for authentic connection and his ability to achieve it.

At Woodhall, we begin not by fixing, but by seeing. We meet each boy where he is, learning his constellation of interests, strengths, areas of growth, and personal history. We discover the patterns of frustration that have shaped his past and the untapped potential waiting to emerge. The journey starts from that meeting point – from a place of recognition and respect – and builds outward. For each student, the opportunities for success look different, yet the process begins with the same foundation: the school's mission.

> *The mission of The Woodhall School is to provide an opportunity for success to young men of above-average intellectual ability in grades 9–12, who have had difficulties in traditional school environments. The school embraces an individualized approach that allows each student to realize his potential and to take accountability in all areas of his life.*

This mission is not a slogan. It serves as a framework for every decision made on campus. It guides faculty hiring, curriculum design, dormitory life, athletics, and even mealtime conversations. The mission is lived, not laminated. Every adult mentor and staff member, from the Head of School to the newest teacher, operates with a unified purpose: to help each student find his own version of success, not someone else's.

Such alignment is made possible by Woodhall's size. With a maximum enrollment of 45 students, the school's scale is intentionally intimate. It allows every adult to know every student – not as a name on a roster, but as an individual with history, humor, and humanity. With the school's structure, every program interlocks; every support overlaps. As stated in the school's motto – *Soli Ipse Adesse* – "Be present to [the student] himself alone" – we ensure that every boy is seen, supported and celebrated.

The late Marcia Rubinstein, educational consultant, author, and Woodhall alumni parent, was fond of the saying: "In order to make a difference, you need to be different."

That difference is nowhere more evident than in Woodhall's Communications Program – the school's defining feature and one of its greatest innovations. The Communications Program is not a single class or meeting. It is an immersive, daily practice of self-reflection, accountability, and interpersonal awareness that shapes the entire culture. It manifests in structured components like School Forum, Committee for Accountability, Communications Groups, and Advisory, but it also lives in hallway conversations, dorm meetings, and quiet moments of reflection after a difficult day. It is how the school turns talk into transformation.

The program is guided by one essential question: *"How do I relate to and respect the perspective of others?"* Over time, students learn to answer that question not through theory but through tangible change – change in language, in tone, in empathy, and ultimately, in action. Each interaction becomes a learning opportunity; each moment of conflict becomes a step toward understanding.

This relationship-based model is at the heart of everything Woodhall does. Faculty are called Adult Mentors rather than teachers, emphasizing the holistic role in students' lives. Fourteen of the school's seventeen mentors live on campus, sharing meals, coaching teams, leading activities, and opening their homes to conversation. Their presence blurs the traditional boundaries between classroom and community, between teacher and guide. In doing so, they create the conditions for real and lasting growth – the kind that happens when learning and living intertwine.

The foundation of this approach draws on restorative practices, a philosophy that emphasizes repair over punishment and dialogue over discipline. Students learn to take accountability for their actions not out of fear of consequence but out of respect for relationships. They understand that their choices ripple outward, affecting others and the community as a whole. By engaging in honest, facilitated dialogue, they develop the tools to resolve conflict and rebuild trust.

This process is not always easy. It demands courage – to face oneself, to admit fault, to speak truth, to listen with humility. But within the safety of Woodhall's culture, that courage grows. As students practice listening and demonstrating empathy, they develop cognitive flexibility, emotional regulation, and resilience. They begin to see confrontation not as something to avoid but as an opportunity to grow.

At Woodhall, the word *confrontation* carries none of its usual negativity. Instead, it is reframed as a meeting, literally a "coming face to face." Through confrontation with integrity, compassion, and respect, students learn to understand both themselves and others more deeply. Listening becomes a tool of connection. Empathy becomes a bridge.

This process of relational learning changes everything. Students who once recoiled from feedback begin to seek it. Those who once deflected responsibility learn to own their actions with humility. Over time, they begin to take ownership of the school's core values of Compassion, Integrity, and Respect not as platitudes, but as daily habits.

As one alumnus from the Class of 2016 reflected, "[Woodhall gave me] the opportunity to shed what was in order to become closer to what I can be."

W. B. Yeats once wrote, "Education is not the filling of a pail but the lighting of a fire."

At The Woodhall School, this reflection resonates deeply – not only as a metaphor but as an active principle of the school's pedagogy. The goal of learning here is not accumulation, but illumination: to invite curiosity, kindle confidence, and inspire lifelong growth.

Woodhall's academic program is structured to provide both scaffolding and stretch – the necessary support for executive functioning development paired with the intellectual challenge that awakens curiosity. Each student follows a comprehensive college preparatory course of study that includes senior electives, independent study projects, and Advanced Placement courses. These academic experiences are deliberately designed to cultivate self-awareness as a learner: to teach *how* to learn, rather than simply *what* to learn.

Class sizes rarely exceed five students. In this intimate setting, every student is known and heard. Multi-modal instruction – combining visual, auditory, and kinesthetic learning – meets students where they are, while still holding them to high expectations. Teachers adapt content delivery, pacing, and assessment to individual learning profiles. For many students, this is the first time that the educational system has adapted to them, rather than the other way around.

The academic day is punctuated by moments of deliberate reflection. Structured evening study hall, a six-day-a-week routine for underclassmen, transforms homework from an isolated struggle into a guided process. Teachers are available each evening for extra help, ensuring that learning doesn't stop at the end of the class day. Seniors, who earn the privilege to study independently, do so having already internalized the structure and accountability that will serve them in college.

Alumni frequently return to campus and tell the current students the same thing: "*Structured study hall works.*" What seems, at first, like a simple routine becomes a foundation for self-discipline. Many alumni describe entering college far more prepared than their peers – not because they memorized more facts, but because they understood how to manage time, seek help, and advocate for themselves.

That advocacy is another outgrowth of Woodhall's Communications Program. Students practice communicating with clarity and confidence, skills that later translate into successful interactions with college professors, employers, and peers. They learn that self-advocacy is not entitlement but empowerment – the ability to articulate needs and take ownership of their own education.

The range of coursework at Woodhall reflects both rigor and creativity. Students might begin the morning analyzing poetry in Advanced Placement English, spend midday wiring circuits in a STEAM lab, and close the day discussing ethical dilemmas in a history seminar.

Laughter and good-natured debate fill the classrooms. It is common to see students lingering after class, continuing a discussion, or an Adult Mentor sitting beside a student, reviewing his essay line by line. That easy familiarity and humorous rapport – what visitors often call the "summer camp feeling" – coexists with genuine academic seriousness.

Woodhall's small size also enables *depth over breadth*. Instead of racing through a standard curriculum, teachers and students take time to go deeper, to question assumptions, and to connect ideas across disciplines. For students who once felt lost in the anonymity of larger schools, this close attention can be transformative.

The school embraces the aphorism from the Roman poet, Juvenal – "Mens sana in corpore sano." A sound mind in a sound body.

The connection between mind and body, between intellect and well-being, marks another central tenet of Woodhall's philosophy. This ideal is expressed through the school's integrated athletics and arts programs, which emphasize creativity, collaboration, and accountability in action. Participation in either an athletic or theatre arts pursuit is required each of the three trimesters. This expectation reinforces balance and commitment: every student is both an academic learner and a contributing member of the community's cultural and physical life.

Woodhall athletes may compete in interscholastic soccer, cross-country, basketball, wrestling, or lacrosse. Other students may choose Outdoor Challenge – a program that includes hiking, canoeing, and rock climbing –

or the award-winning Woodhall Players theater troupe. Regardless of their choice, participation is active, immersive, and character-building.

The Phoenix, Woodhall's mascot, symbolizes renewal and transformation. It represents not only the individual student's journey but the collective spirit of the community. Whether gathered around a bonfire after a cross-country meet or warming up for rehearsal in the Abigail J. Woodhall Theatre, students and Adult Mentors share in that same ethos: rising from challenge, creating something new, and taking pride in growth.

Athletics at Woodhall may be small in scale but not in spirit. With a student body of only 45, nearly every boy participates, and the diversity of ability is celebrated. There are varsity athletes who compete at NEPSAC championships and newcomers who are picking up a lacrosse stick or wearing a wrestling singlet for the first time. Each discovers the satisfaction of teamwork, effort, and perseverance.

For many students, the athletic field becomes a parallel classroom. They learn lessons about trust, communication, and humility that mirror the principles taught in the Communications Program. Losing a game becomes a chance to model accountability. Winning becomes an opportunity to practice grace.

For those drawn to the outdoors rather than competition, Outdoor Challenge offers a different kind of rigor. Students canoe on local lakes and rivers, learn basic survival and navigation skills, and culminate each season with a hike to the summit of Bear Mountain, the highest point in Connecticut. Standing at the peak, surveying the Litchfield Hills and the Taconic and Berkshire Mountains and beyond, they experience a moment of literal and metaphorical perspective - a reminder of how far they've climbed, both physically and personally.

The arts program, meanwhile, provides its own form of ascent. The Woodhall Players produce two major theatrical productions each year in the

Abigail J. Woodhall Theatre, a remarkable feat for a community of 45 high school boys. The winter and spring plays are community-wide events, attended by families, alumni, and local supporters. Over the past two decades, the Players have been repeatedly nominated for - and have won - statewide Halo Awards for excellence in secondary school theater.

Theater at Woodhall is more than performance; it is personal transformation. Students who once dreaded public speaking discover the thrill of self-expression. Shy students may find their voices in ensemble work. Through rehearsal, improvisation, and shared vulnerability, they learn collaboration, emotional awareness, and the courage to take risks. Retired faculty member Tony Sherer, who was instrumental in building the drama program, once reflected:

> *For the most part, boys came to Woodhall to escape an unsuccessful experience elsewhere. Since many adolescents are uncomfortable in their rapidly changing selves, Woodhall – and drama in particular – gave them a legitimate opportunity to reinvent themselves for a while. In the safety of an experience which required the best of everybody, individual kids could disappear into a task greater than themselves. Several had never considered the stage before and found a new home there.*

Those words capture a truth that extends beyond the stage. Every classroom, field, and studio at Woodhall is a stage for reinvention. Each space invites students to try, to fail, to try again – to rediscover themselves through action. Whether it is solving an equation in Calculus, throwing a discus on the athletic field, or crafting a ceramic bowl in the art studio, the act of doing becomes the catalyst for becoming.

This balance of rigor, reflection, and relationship defines the Woodhall experience. Academic challenge meets emotional growth; structure meets empathy; accountability meets compassion. It is a place where a boy who once said "I can't" begins to realize, step by step, that he can.

If Woodhall's classrooms and playing fields are laboratories of learning, then its dormitories are the heart of community life. It is within these living spaces that theory becomes practice - where lessons about responsibility, respect, and empathy unfold in real time.

The residential program at The Woodhall School is not merely an adjunct to the academic day; it is an extension of the educational mission. Life in the dorms teaches students to coexist, to manage themselves, and to live with purpose. Adult Mentors – faculty who live in residence – guide students through the rhythms of daily life, offering both structure and support.

The dorms are intentionally personal. There are shared responsibilities – cleaning schedules, common-area upkeep, and nightly check-ins – that cultivate accountability. Students quickly learn that community requires contribution.

Evening hours at Woodhall follow a structured cadence: family-style dinner in the dining hall, followed by the all-important study hall, and then time for relaxation, conversation, or recreation. Faculty members are ever-present, available not only for academic help, but also for guidance, humor, and listening. Over time, the relationship between student and mentor evolves from supervision to mentorship, and finally, to mutual respect.

It is not unusual to see an older student helping a younger student, or a faculty member walking with a student by the pond, talking through the day's successes and frustrations. These small, repeated moments define the culture of Woodhall. They represent the consistent, intentional attention that transforms potential into confidence.

One of Woodhall's long-standing traditions, Student Leadership, is, in many ways, an extension of the Communications Program. Student Leaders serve as liaisons between students and adult mentors and help plan social activities. Leadership is framed not as authority, but as service.

Student Leaders model the process of developing skills of self-reflection and self-expression with accountability for other students. Ultimately, every student can experience a leadership role, whether formally as Student Leader or informally as a peer mentor.

Service to others is woven into the fabric of school life. Students participate in local volunteer projects, including food drives, environmental cleanups, and community events in the surrounding towns of Litchfield County.

The daily Morning Morning is another ritual that connects the community. We begin each day with a mindfulness practice and then share announcements, celebrate achievements, and reflect on the day ahead. These gatherings begin and end with gratitude, often punctuated by humor, spontaneous applause, and moments of insight.

The physical campus itself reinforces the school's intimate scale. Surrounded by rolling woodlands and rambling stone walls, the architecture blends buildings of barn-like simplicity with state-of-the art learning and community spaces. The campus evokes both history and purpose. There is a rhythm to life here, marked by the change of classes, the echo of activity on Phoenix Field or Trevor's Pond, and the laughter of boys spilling from the dining hall after dinner. The setting reflects the school's deeper mission: to offer peace without complacency, connection without confrontation, and rigor without rigidity.

That mission can be traced directly to the vision of its founders, Mrs. Sally Campbell Woodhall and Dr. Jonathan A. Woodhall, who established the school in 1983. Their shared conviction was that education must serve the whole person – intellectual, emotional, physical, and spiritual. They sought to create an environment that was structured and humane, where boys could recover from educational setbacks and discover their inner strength.

Founding Head of School, Sally Woodhall, brought to the endeavor an acute understanding of what many schools lacked: empathy, flexibility, and belief in human potential. The Woodhall School exists for "the boy who has not yet found his success." That phrase, simple yet profound, continues to define the institution. It speaks to the belief that each student is more than a label, that his capacity for growth and connection comes from within himself.

The founders rejected the idea that academic remediation or behavioral modification could solve the struggles of students who had faltered elsewhere. Instead, they designed a school that would attend to self-concept – the way a young man understands himself in relation to learning, community, and purpose.

This focus on identity development – on helping students articulate who they are and what they value – remains the foundation of the Woodhall experience. Adult mentors work not only as teachers but as partners in self-discovery. Each interaction, each challenge, and each success is framed as an opportunity for reflection.

Alumni often speak of Woodhall as the place where they first felt "seen." Many arrived skeptical and guarded, carrying the weight of academic disappointment or social alienation. Over time, through mentorship, structure, and community, they began to rewrite their internal narratives.

One alumnus from the Class of 1995 described the transformation poignantly:

> *At Woodhall, I learned how to take myself seriously. Before, I thought being smart was about getting good grades. Here, I realized it's about showing up for others, doing the work of building relationships, and being honest when you make a mistake. I left knowing that success isn't about being perfect – it's about having the courage to keep going.*

The goal is not perfection, but progress. The school values authenticity over polish, growth over performance. The result is a culture where vulnerability is not weakness, but the starting point for resilience. Alumni describe a lifelong connection to the place and to the people who shaped their journey. An alumni parent recalls her son's experience:

> *Woodhall boys often need a re-set. They've experienced negative feedback often their entire lives. These "layers of mud" accumulate and negative self-affect sets in. Likely there are patterns that need to change at home and out in the world – even when families are making their best attempts. The Woodhall School provides the reset. They get in the mud and help your child chip away at those layers. Their Communications program helped our son develop perspective taking and perspective understanding. He learned that the adults at the Woodhall School wouldn't give up on him and he sees his years at Woodhall as a gift – to get back to his true self that was hidden away beneath all those layers. There's a process at Woodhall – they encourage families to "trust the process" and they know what they're doing. They enrich, accelerate, and support where needed and they lean into our child's strengths.*

The holistic outcome is not incidental – it is intentional. The Woodhall model demonstrates that academic excellence and emotional intelligence are not competing, but rather, complementary goals. By cultivating both, the school sends forth graduates who are capable of navigating life's complexities with confidence, humility, and integrity.

Now in its fifth decade, The Woodhall School continues to evolve without losing sight of its roots. It is important to note the school's improbable beginnings. By most objective measures, The Woodhall School wasn't likely to survive. The school opened in the autumn of 1983 without much to show for it: five students, five teachers, a smattering of modular buildings, an aging farmhouse, and very little money.

Yet, over the years, we at Woodhall believed in and were present to every boy. We didn't give up on them, even when so many of them had already given up on themselves. In our work with the students, we have led with our core values of integrity, compassion, and respect. We have stayed true to the mission. We have stayed true to the boys. As with the young men to whom we have been present, whom we have encouraged, whom we have held accountable – and, above all, whom we have loved – the school itself and the community it represents became a Phoenix rising from ashes, creating lasting light, warmth, and hope from within. Woodhall has worked, and works, for the boys we serve.

Riverview School

Location: East Sandwich, Massachusetts

Year Founded: 1957

Grades Served: 6–12 + Post Grad (GROW) + Friend Forever (Ages 22+)

Total Enrollment: 197

Percent Boarding: 83%

Percent Non-White: 13%

Percent From Out of State: 40%

Percent From Out of Country: 6%

2025–26 School Year Tuition: $113,491

Percent Who Receive Financial Aid: 80%

School Website: www.riverviewschool.org

Head of School: Executive Director, Stewart Miller; Head of Middle and High School, Deanna White; Head of GROW, Charlie McNamara

Riverview School

Chapter Completed By

Annalise Yurgelun, Marketing and Communications Manager

Cape Cod is known for its lighthouses. Quiet, unwavering sentinels that shine through fog and storm, guiding weary travelers safely to shore. They stand not only as a beacon of light, but as a symbol of hope, especially for those who feel lost at sea. Its mission is simple: it's to lead us home. Riverview is one such lighthouse; where every student, no matter the tide they've weathered, can chart a course forward, and where every family, no matter the worry, can find the same, steady light, guiding them home.

– Justin Gray, Riverview Alum
Sibling and Board of Trustees Member

The journey to Riverview often starts with a conversation in a doctor's office. A classroom. Maybe a friend's birthday party. A missed developmental milestone that leads to a quiet concern that keeps a parent up at night. For many Riverview families, this is only the beginning of a long road to finding our School, as it is in that moment that everything changes. What once seemed like a typical childhood now holds questions and uncertainty. No blog, book, or newsletter can prepare them for the weight of that realization: it's them and their child, navigating a world that doesn't always make room for difference. It is the unexpected start of a lifelong journey that they never imagined taking.

A medical, neurological, or communication diagnosis is only the first step, as these limitations in development and independence can lead to isolation from peers and a tendency to be overlooked in educational, social, and everyday environments. The focus shifts to "fixing what's wrong" rather than developing personal passions or recognizing strengths and abilities. Families can often see their child's capabilities better than anyone else, putting them in a position of having to push back and become the ultimate advocate for their child's potential, and their right to be appreciated for who they truly are. Even school districts, the institutions created to educate and protect children, sometimes cannot provide satisfactory services, hindering basic educational foundations for children with higher needs.

At Riverview, a school for students with complex language, learning, and cognitive challenges, we understand what many families are searching for: a place where their child is not only supported but truly seen, valued, and empowered. Often internally called "The *True* Happiest Place On Earth" among families and staff, students shine as their differences aren't seen as something to shy away from. They are no longer pulled out of the classroom, no longer sitting on the sidelines of the basketball game, and no longer struggling to find their social circle.

Upon first glance, Riverview seems like a classic New England independent boarding and day school, with its state-of-the-art buildings, smiling staff and students, and beautiful campus. However, underneath this familiar "boarding school" surface lies a mission deeply focused on each individual. Riverview offers a robust range of programming to fit the needs of our Middle-High School students, and also provides an additional program for post-secondary students called "GROW," or "Getting Ready for the Outside World." GROW acts as a college campus of sorts, with students increasing their vocational hours and learning advanced independent living skills alongside Functional Academics. At its core, Riverview was designed to foster competence and confidence across academics, social development, and autonomy within our students. An even closer look would quickly reveal that what happens on the Riverview campus is nothing short of miraculous.

So, here lies the question: what, exactly, does Riverview do differently that creates these miracles?

Riverview's mixture of an innovative curriculum designed around educating the Whole Student, as well as increased programming for families and alumni, creates an educational model of support unlike any other. Here, every student is recognized as an individual with unique strengths, needs, and dreams. They are given a voice in shaping their own aspirations, and families are embraced as essential partners in the journey. Our team of dedicated staff members works closely with students and families to provide the right balance of structure, assistance, challenge, and opportunity, ensuring each student grows academically, socially, emotionally, and strengthens even their everyday life skills. It's more than a school, it's a community that believes in every child, celebrates all student progress, and prepares them to lead a life filled with purpose, belonging, and joy.

Riverview's curriculum is rooted in the belief that students with complex learning and cognitive disabilities are capable of accomplishing remarkable things when in the right environment. When looking at the progress made every day on campus and the lifelong successes our students have had, there's no denying that, with a dedicated program formulated to promote independence, confidence, and skills, our students can accomplish anything they put their minds to. Our professional staff members are not just trained to teach, but are also united by a commitment to provide the best possible environment for our students to gain skills and find the strength within themselves to live their best lives.

Riverview has developed an innovative **Whole-Student Philosophy** that consists of five core competencies that, when integrated into a comprehensive curriculum, best foster whole-student growth. The core competencies are Educational Growth, Social Emotional Skills, Wellness, Independent Living, and Vocational Readiness. The whole student approach provides a balance of building skills and strategies with encouraging students to awaken their individual talents, discover their passions, and find what they love. It provides foundational components that promote long-term success.

Education

In speaking with staff and families, it's not uncommon to hear the phrase "*Riverview meets students where they're at.*" But, when it comes to **Education**, what does that mean exactly? Prior to enrolling, our students have typically had 1:1 or pull-out services, with some spending entire school days in a separate room from their peers. Once stepping foot on our campus, that is never the case. All services happen within the walls of the classroom, ensuring that students receive the full school experience alongside their classmates. But, it doesn't stop there, as one of the most impressive things about our programming is our commitment to age-appropriate education. Riverview high school students read texts such as *Beowulf* and *The Count of Monte Cristo*, just like other high school students their age. While the text is modified for every student's needs, the content remains the same and allows them to have the appropriate exposure to academic topics. We have also formulated a ground-breaking curriculum that allows for real-world application built into the classroom and on campus. Teachers utilize Functional Academics (classes that serve a greater purpose than the lesson at hand); Math classes become budgeting, and learning how to open and manage a bank account. Theater class turns into improv, running scenarios of working in a coffee shop or navigating a social event. "Education" doesn't stop at academics, either. Our students are constantly learning in all areas of school life. Dorms have adapted curriculum to promote independence and skill development, and recreational activities are viewed as teaching experiences; students are even learning in the dining hall as they interact with staff and peers.

There is no "Whole Student" without fostering creativity and personal growth within the individual through enrichment courses. Riverview encourages students to explore their interests and think outside the box with our well-rounded arts and music programming, hands-on classroom experiences, field trips, and more. For many students, these enrichment opportunities build confidence and self-assuredness that they may not have discovered otherwise. The student actor, once relegated to the supporting cast, now has the opportunity to sing as the lead in the play. A student rock band regularly takes the stage, encouraged by their peers cheering in the audience, and artwork proudly graces the academic hallways. Based on trending interests, Riverview will adjust the enrichment curriculum to encourage a high-quality educational environment that will promote lifelong learning; for example, we recently added a highly requested podcast and broadcasting class, and added cheerleading to our list of afternoon activities. The primary focus in all areas of education remains on providing guidance towards the most fulfilling path for each individual, and encouraging confidence to fully explore all Riverview has to offer.

Social Emotional:

> *The warmth and acceptance that she enjoys here have allowed her to blossom.*
>
> – Riverview Parent

Success at Riverview isn't just about education and academics; it's about learning to navigate the world with resilience, confidence, and a sense of belonging. **Social Emotional** well-being is essential for our students to learn to assess situations, manage their emotions, and respond to adversity with strength and self-awareness. And while big achievements matter, it's often the quieter moments that show the most profound growth. Moments such as dancing at a school dance for the first time, winning a medal at the Special Olympics, or laughing with friends at lunch. For some families, this might seem ordinary. For ours, it's everything.

These small but powerful milestones are the ones that show just how far a student has come in their own personal journey. Riverview celebrates progress in every form, and we understand that emotional growth is not only possible, but transformative.

Wellness:

> *We imagined how amazing it would be to teach our students to calm their minds, center their bodies, and ultimately lift their spirits*
>
> – Riverview Teacher

> *Wellness is a huge priority because a good number of our students may have a higher likelihood of developing chronic diseases as they get older... what we want to do is provide*

them an opportunity here where they can learn a foundation of living a healthy life, to set them up for success.

– Nicole Larizza, Riverview's Nutrition Specialist

Through physical fitness, nutrition, and mindfulness, Riverview incorporates **Wellness** into every student's day-to-day life. Our state-of-the-art Wellness Center is home to an updated fitness center, full gym, indoor track, and exercise equipment. A wide range of classes makes sure that students find what they truly enjoy. From dance, spin, and boxing to mindfulness and yoga, classes focus on personal improvement and finding fun in exercise. Our athletic teams compete in the Special Olympics and against other schools in the area. The newest wellness endeavor includes the Nutrition Center, which includes a learning space, as well as multiple updated kitchen workstations. Here, students learn the values of nutrition and building a meal from scratch that is full of nutrients, but tastes delicious.

In order to achieve this goal of wellness from the inside out, Riverview has a dedicated "Wellness" staff, whose primary focus is to encourage life-long habits for healthy living. There is not just a gym teacher, but a well-trained group of educators dedicated to Wellness. Riverview's Nutrition Specialist equips students with the knowledge and skill to build a healthy meal from scratch, and teaches about what it really means to have a balanced diet. In all areas of wellness, Riverview encourages students to find what works best for them and equips them with the tools to create their own sustainable, healthy lifestyle.

Independent Living:

Promoting strong **Independent Living Skills** is a critical part of our educational model. We are proud to say that in a poll of recently graduated students, we have found that 64% of recent graduates reported living outside their family home (some supported in a supported living program, and others independently). For families of neurotypical children, the concept of a post-education life may look like an internship, an apartment with friends, or taking exercise classes. That is not the reality for many parents of neurodivergent families, as they are tasked early on with the constant thought of "*what comes next*?" Because of this, Riverview has structured dorm settings with their own curriculum, as students learn about social skills, responsibility, and time management, all under the oversight of a dedicated and trained staff. Students are guided through daily routines that emphasize the importance of self-care and personal hygiene, helping them take ownership of their health and well-being. Additional independence skills, such as travel training, grocery shopping, and needs vs. wants budgeting, ensure that students are equipped with vital everyday living tools before they navigate the world on their own.

Vocational:

With our wide range of community partnerships, Riverview is proud to support students in a variety of **Vocational** opportunities. Students have the opportunity to work in the hospitality industry at one of the Cape's beautiful seaside resorts, ring up customers in local coffee shops, and assist with stocking shelves at stores. Riverview also owns two local businesses, Cafe Riverview and Second View Thrift Store. These establishments act as a vocational classroom for students to learn in a safe, welcoming environment, and they help local community members get to know our school. A partnership with the internationally acclaimed Project SEARCH (A nonprofit that facilitates internships and learning experiences in large-scale businesses for young adults with intellectual and developmental disabilities) at Cape Cod Healthcare gives students the opportunity to gain experience in rotating healthcare positions. From the front desk to organizing the necessary supplies for the ER, students who are a part of this program see the day-to-day work within a healthcare environment, and many go on to continue careers within the field. All vocational roles in GROW are tailored to each student's strengths to promote confidence, as well as encourage participation in a fulfilling and sustainable career post-graduation. In fact, 75% of Riverview graduates reported that they are working in competitive job settings, which is five times the national rate for adults with Intellectual and Developmental Disabilities (IDD).

"*This is what freedom looks like.*" – Riverview Parent

For many people, the word "school" evokes the mental image of a classroom. Pencils, books, desks, maybe a shiny red apple. But if asked about what they remember from their school years, rarely does anyone tell stories of sitting in math class. The memories are full of friendships, prom, and winning the "big game." At Riverview, we focus on curriculum, yes, but a large part of our educational model also goes to providing our students with the same traditional experiences. Our staff members are trained to work with each student and show them the genuine respect that they deserve, effectively allowing students autonomy over their own lives and giving them access to adolescent milestones. Our students are winning medals at the Special Olympics Track and Field Meet, dancing with friends at the Friday night dance, taking the stage to perform with their rock band, and playing the lead in the school play. While these may seem like small victories to some, they are the moments that truly change the trajectory of our students' lives and provide families with a deep sense of relief and renewed joy. Families are able to put those days of sitting and wondering aside for a moment and breathe, as they witness their children find confidence in who they are, and transform their differences into superpowers, instead of something to be "fixed" or "worked around." This, above all else, sets Riverview apart from the rest. With no reservations, students who at one time were allocated to the back of the stage are now singing front and center, while their peers cheer them on from the audience. They're picking out prom dresses with friends on the weekend, and trying new activities they'd never thought of before. It's not uncommon for our students to join the local assisted hockey league, even if they've never even skated before. Activities such as weekend ski trips to Vermont and Swim Team welcome students at every level, helping beginners gain confidence and explore new challenges. Riverview provides a buoy, so there is no fear of sinking; they're given the opportunity (some for the first time) to take their own wants and needs into account, and build confidence and self-advocacy to enjoy these formative years and find out who they really are.

Through all of these experiences, the peer support for one another and overall student culture is second to none. When it comes to our students, their classmates will only cheer them on louder, congratulate them more, and encourage them to try again when it comes to stepping outside their comfort zone. While many of our students have only ever experienced ostracization from other children their own age, they finally get to experience true friendship. During school breaks, families have reported the happy shock of finding out that their student is now on a large group chat with their friends, they need a ride to a classmate's birthday party, or that they can't wait to get back to school so they can catch up with their roommate. In a world where the number one predictor of adult happiness relies on strong, supportive relationships (as shown in the Harvard Study of Adult Development), these friendships are critical to ensuring positive growth and lifelong happiness within our students and alumni.

Once students arrive at Riverview and start flourishing, the trajectory of the journey takes a turn, and the families' focus has to adjust based on the ever-changing success and growth of their child. Because of these realities, they are required to always be thinking about the next steps; every family faces their own triumphs and challenges as they head toward the unknown after Riverview. As a result, we place a high importance on not just our educational model for students, but Family Education and Support. This programming offers the opportunity to build strong foundations within the community and provide families with the tools for navigating their child's newfound independence, especially navigating the large leap after they graduate. Much like our student population, many families have felt isolated from their peers. However, now a part of Riverview, they find themselves joining a community of other families who have shared experiences.

Throughout the school year, Riverview hosts Family Education Seminars, book clubs, and webinars. Families are encouraged to make connections at school events, as certain activities and informational sessions are reserved as networking opportunities. A large piece of this puzzle includes the siblings, as the reality is that a sibling of a child with developmental differences plays a significant role in the family. A Sibling Support Panel and Sibling Social Reception at Riverview's Fall Family Weekend introduces them to one another to build a support system beyond Riverview. Targeted book clubs and group events encourage family discussions among parents and siblings of Riverview students, providing a foundation of open communication for all. Once a student graduates, families still have opportunities to connect via virtual alumni discussions and events, as well.

At this point in the journey, one has to ask - what next? With all of the structured support provided on campus, what do students do after they walk across the graduation stage?

Thanks to a transformative donation, Riverview is building "Friends Forever," an intentional membership-based program that extends the promise of our school into adulthood. Anchored by a centralized community center located in Hyannis, a short walk from a busy Main Street and accessible by public transportation, Friends Forever is designed first for Riverview alumni, but also welcomes the broader Cape area through reverse integration, inviting members into public-facing programs while preserving dedicated spaces and services for members. Alumni will register for classes and small-group activities across wellness, arts, music, recreation, independent living, and continuing education; drop in to welcoming spaces to relax, meet friends, and join informal activities; and gather on evenings and weekends for performances, game nights, dances, and celebrations. Friends Forever helps members explore new interests and deepen longstanding passions, and over time, will add individualized supports that foster friendships and provide pathways to employment. Looking ahead, the campus will also include housing for alumni and public amenities such as a gym, a general store, a working farm, and parkland with walking trails. While the campus is in early development with pilot programming already underway, we are targeting a summer 2027 opening, with subsequent phases adding residential options and additional public-facing assets. With the founding of Friends Forever, Riverview is creating a longitudinal model of education, support, and connection, from adolescence to adulthood, for people with complex language, learning, and cognitive differences. It will no longer be the case that Riverview students need to find a new community once they graduate from the school.

It can be hard to think back to the start of the journey mentioned earlier, as that family, witnessing the missed developmental milestone, had no way to picture what the future would look like for their loved one. However, by Graduation Day, that uncertainty changes to possibility. Neurotypical students don't build their futures around remedying weakness, and neither should our students. Riverview is filled with exploring passions, strengths, and talents, and we provide them with the tools to maintain this self-assurance long after leaving. Students go on to pursue a happy, fulfilled existence that maintains much-deserved respect. Every Riverview student has a myriad of talents to share with the world, and deserves to have the opportunity to explore everything they can in order to find a foundation for professional and personal happiness. At Riverview, we give students much more than an education; we give the gift of a life reimagined.

"Don't judge. Just be." – Riverview Student

St. Johnsbury Academy

Location: St. Johnsbury, Vermont

Year Founded: 1842

Grades Served: 9–12 + Post Grad

Total Enrollment: 950

Percent Boarding: 20%

Percent Non-White: 10%

Percent From Out of State: 12%

Percent From Out of Country: 15%

2025–26 School Year Tuition: $72,700

Percent Who Receive Financial Aid: 85%

School Website: www.stjacademy.org

Head of School: Sharon Howell

St. Johnsbury Academy

Submission Completed By
Nicole Biggie, Director of Admission & Tammi Cady, Assistant Head for Advancement

St. Johnsbury Academy is a unique place and so refreshing to me. Down to earth and comfortable, no airs and yet prideful, talented, multi-faceted, and creative. The sense of community is strong there. I miss being a part of a community like this where truly the whole is bigger than the parts measured in a soulful, non status way.

– Peter, Educational Consultant

History – Over 180 Years

St. Johnsbury Academy (SJA), an independent day and boarding school in St. Johnsbury, Vermont, was founded in 1842 by the three Fairbanks brothers Erastus, Joseph, and Thaddeus, "to provide intellectual, moral, and religious training" for their own children and those of the community.

SJA's history represents a long march towards inclusion, with its mission expanded several times in order to better meet the needs of its students and the community. From the start, the Fairbanks family's financial support – they were inventors of and manufactured the first platform scales – kept tuition low enough that any qualified student could attend. In 1873, the school was reincorporated to accomplish the founder's expanded goal of providing exemplary educational opportunities to a wider range of students, not just those destined for college.

In establishing SJA, the founders sought to create an institution that would cultivate the heart and hand as well as the mind, inspire thinking beyond mere acquisition of knowledge, and develop morally and intellectually self-reliant citizens. By offering a uniquely relevant and comprehensive education to each student and committing to providing the support necessary to help each student become a successful communicator, problem solver, and citizen, St. Johnsbury Academy has remained true to its historic mission.

SJA enrolled both boarding and day students from its inception. Boarding students have played an important role in school life since the school's founding, and their influence has expanded as their numbers and international diversity have grown. SJA is also one of the only New England Academies that has always educated both girls and boys.

Unlike most other independent schools, the Academy has achieved success while maintaining its commitment to serving the educational needs of each student from the local community. Vermont has a long history of school choice, dating back to 1777 when its constitution mandated public schools in each town. The "town tuitioning" program, established in 1869, is the oldest in the nation, allowing students in towns without public high schools to attend public or private schools elsewhere, with the sending town covering the tuition.

Today, St. Johnsbury Academy is a vibrant day and boarding school of 950 students, perched atop 50 scenic acres in the Northeast Kingdom of Vermont. Our location on Main Street in the town of St. Johnsbury puts students within easy walking distance of a variety of restaurants, theaters, several art galleries, and the Fairbanks Museum and Planetarium. Skiing and some of the best mountain biking trails in the country are less than one-half hour away. St. Johnsbury and Vermont are consistently ranked at the top of national lists for safety and outdoor adventure. SJA has been recognized by the United States Department of Education as an exemplary private school, while at the same time gaining both a national and international reputation as a model for community-wide education.

Combining the resources, facilities, and extensive curricular and extracurricular offerings of the nation's leading independent schools with the personal attention, small class size, and support of the best small boarding schools, SJA has attracted an extraordinarily diverse student body. The school now serves around 750 day students from St. Johnsbury and 50 surrounding towns in Vermont and New Hampshire and 200 boarding students from over a dozen states and more than 20 countries. Within a small, rural Vermont town lies an international, metropolitan, culturally diverse group of students spanning the socioeconomic spectrum living and learning together.

At the heart of SJA lies a mission grounded in Character, Inquiry, and Community. Guided by deep optimism about young people, three promises are made to students and their families:

1. To help each student become the best person possible.

We are committed to the values of respect, compassion, integrity, and responsibility. We have compassion and empathy, and we believe in loving those most who need it most.

2. To become the best learner possible.

We value expertise, creativity, and the habit of inquiry. We provide support and opportunities for students to pursue their passions and develop an abiding love for learning.

3. Become part of something bigger than themselves.

When students come to St. Johnsbury Academy, they become part of the most talented and diverse group of individuals they may ever know as friends and colleagues. They develop an intellectual and emotional connection to understanding the larger world, and to making the community a better place.

Campus – beautiful and safe

Arriving on campus, students and families are in awe of its beauty. Traditional academic buildings and houses from the early years of the school are interspersed with more modern facilities, all ranged among wide open lawns and trees that glow with color in the fall. The most recent physical additions to campus are the Charles Hosmer Morse Center for the Arts, and the Mayo Center. The Morse Arts Center consists of six fine arts studios, an art gallery, a print and photography studio, two music performance studios with five practice rooms, a dance studio, and a 200-seat black box theater. The Mayo Center, with floor-to-ceiling windows overlooking campus from both floors, houses the Grace Stuart Orcutt library with 20,000 volumes, private and small group study spaces, and a media presentation room. The building is also home to the Colwell Center for Global Understanding and a student lounge. In the planning phase, and expected to open in 2027, is a new and renovated center for student life, athletics, and health and wellness programs.

Academics – for all learners

St. Johnsbury Academy offers a rigorous and multi-level academic program that blends traditional college preparatory education with innovative, hands-on learning experiences. With over 200 courses, including

Advanced Placement (32), honors, fine arts, world languages, environmental sustainability, and technical education options, SJA caters to a wide range of student interests and aspirations. Each SJA student completes a capstone project in a chosen field in their senior year. The wide range of offerings is reflected in our Signature Programs:

AP Capstone Diploma

SJA is on a short list of schools worldwide that offers this program. Students who complete the AP Seminar and Research courses earning scores of three or higher on the subsequent exams, as well as on at least four other AP exams, will earn the AP Capstone Diploma, recognizing their demonstration of college-level research, collaboration, and communication skills.

Applied Science and STEM Intensive

This program allows students to focus on three distinct pathways, through both classes and extra-curricular opportunities. Engineering Design and Development, Biomedical and Health Science, and Sustainability Studies concentrations give STEM focused students an exceptional introduction to and strong foundation for their future studies.

International Travel and Cultural Exchange

The Colwell Center for Global Understanding at SJA fosters global education. The Colwell Center coordinates diversity programs, cultural events, international exchange programs, and many student trips abroad each year. We also have a partnership program with our sister school in South Korea, St. Johnsbury Academy Jeju.

Post-Calculus Mathematics

Beyond AP Calculus, AP Statistics, or AP Computer Science classes, particularly motivated students may continue to Multivariable Calculus and Linear Algebra, and further through our partnership with Dartmouth College's high school access program.

SJA Arts Intensive

Our course structure allows art students to take either a wide range of classes for a broad artistic experience or to concentrate their study in one medium for three or four semesters – engaging fully – for an in-depth experience. The SJA Arts Intensive is available in both our visual and performing arts courses: Anatomy and Figure Drawing, Printmaking, Photography, Fashion Design, Filmmaking, Digital Design, Clay, Sculpture, Water-based and Oil Painting. Performing Art classes include: Acting, Stagecraft, Ballet, Modern Dance, Popular Dance, Band, Jazz Band, Chorus, Strings, and Guitar.

SJA Technical Career Intensive

St. Johnsbury Academy differs from other schools in many ways, and one of the most compelling is access to our award-winning technical education program. Whether a student is planning to seek work or further education in a technical field or plans to attend college, they are able to take courses within our Career and Technical Education career clusters: Agriculture, Food, and Natural Resources; Architecture/Construction; Business and Management; Hospitality and Tourism; Human Services; and Transportation, Distribution, and Logistics. In addition to classrooms, this department has workshops for students to exhibit practical training.

Within several of these clusters, students can pursue our SJA Technical Career Intensive: a program that allows interested students to delve deeply into a single area of study. As they work through their chosen Technical Career Intensive Concentration, students obtain impressive experience and credentials that translate into a competitive edge in future study or the pursuit of a career.

Academic Support – meeting students where they are

Our commitment to academic excellence is reflected in small class sizes, individualized instruction, and a faculty deeply dedicated to student growth. Whether pursuing STEM, the humanities, or the arts, students are encouraged to explore deeply, think critically, and prepare thoughtfully for college and career success in a supportive, intellectually rich environment.

In order to meet students where they are, whether the start of their high school career or the end, SJA has support built in for all students and personalized learning support for students with identified learning challenges. From the first day, each student is assigned a faculty advisor. **Advisories** are small groups of students from the same class year who meet together multiple times a week throughout the four-year high school career. The advisor is one of many adults on campus who advocate for students around small questions and larger issues. The advisory program creates immediate connections, a sense of belonging, and helps a large school feel small.

All students benefit from **daily conference period** when teachers remain in their classrooms after school for one-on-one meetings; and the **Learning Center** is open throughout the school day for students to access academic support during their study halls from teachers in a variety of subject areas.

The **Guided Studies** program offers the highest level of learning support. In place of a daily study hall, students receive direct instruction to build skills using their current academic coursework as the vehicle.

In addition, our health center has three full-time mental counselors on staff for scheduled meetings and drop-in social-emotional support. For many students, this opens up the opportunity to be at a comprehensive school with extracurricular activities while still receiving the support they need.

> *I attended two other private schools before finding St. Johnsbury Academy. I was unmotivated, struggling with depression, and my grades reflected it. Everything changed when I enrolled in the Guided Studies program at SJA. It gave me the academic support I needed, but more importantly, it helped me build the confidence I had been missing. My grades improved, I became more active and healthier, and I even performed in the school musical – something the 'old me' never would have imagined doing. SJA supported me in all aspects of my life and it made all the difference.*
>
> – Ryan '24

Athletics and Extracurricular Activities – learning outside the classroom

Outside of the classroom, **athletics and extracurricular life** is a cornerstone of our community, with roughly 40–45% of students actively engaged in at least one of the over 40 interscholastic teams, including Vermont Division I football, soccer, basketball, skiing, lacrosse, cross-country, wrestling, gymnastics, cheerleading, and hockey. Our newly established bowling and E-sports teams have generated a lot of excitement, and our Mountain Bike Club rides and practices at Kingdom Trails – known for some of the best trails in the country. Anchored by top-tier facilities, the athletic program emphasizes excellence, character, and community.

Beyond sports, students can choose from over 60 clubs and leadership groups – ranging from Model UN, Science Olympiad, and Robotics to Outing Club, Drama, and National Honor Society – and participate in service opportunities, student government, theatre productions, and an acclaimed FIRST Robotics team. Recently added is our **X-block** which allows students the opportunity to earn after-school credit to experience faculty interest-driven, non-traditional classes such as American sign language or "Introductory Barista."

With a philosophy that extracurriculars are an extension of academics – promoting resilience, sportsmanship, and lifelong skill-building – students balance rigorous training with teamwork, leadership, and school spirit, whether battling on the field or collaborating on creative and civic initiatives.

Community

St. Johnsbury Academy's rich traditions weave together a sense of belonging, school spirit, and community across generations. Each day begins with Chapel – a school-wide morning assembly where advisory groups gather to affirm values like respect and "leave this place better than you found it." Led by the headmaster and student body president, Chapel provides an opportunity for the entire student body, faculty, and staff to start the day together. From hearing announcements, listening to guest speakers, and celebrating accomplishments, this tradition remains strong because we value the time spent together as a whole school community. It is also during this time that we enforce a dress code that gives students the opportunity to practice individuality while helping them to make choices that also model respect for oneself and those around them in a neat, clean, and appropriate manner.

Pep Chapel launches weekend athletic festivities in the fall, leading into **Homecoming** and "The Game," the storied football rivalry with Lyndon Institute dating back to 1894, complete with class floats, parade, bonfire, and cheering crowds. New students participate in Freshman Sing, performing the Alma Mater to an upperclass audience – a rite of passage that cements their membership. Seasonal celebrations include **Winter Carnival**, a spirited mix of indoor and outdoor contests, and **Spring Day**, a campus-wide festival to welcome warmer weather and signal the coming end to the school year. In spring, fashion students showcase their creations in the annual **Spring Fashion Show**, and seniors culminate their time at the Academy by presenting **Capstone** projects to peers, faculty, and the wider community. **Community service** whether in clubs, classes, or as a school, is an expectation. From daily rituals to grand annual events, these traditions knit students, families, and alumni into a caring community.

Boarding Life

For our boarding students, life on campus fosters a warm, globally minded living-learning community where dorms – from historic mansions to eco-friendly buildings – become close-knit homes. Around 200 boarders – representing many U.S. states and countries – live under the care of dedicated dorm parents who serve as mentors, supervise study hall, and host regular dorm meetings, family-style dinners, and outings throughout the year. With support and structured routines, students not only thrive academically but also build empathy and lifelong friendships across diverse cultures. Orientation in August ensures smooth transitions, and weekend trips – ranging from wilderness excursions to shopping or cultural outings – add adventure and balance to campus life. Our connection to the local community means our boarding students are not just part of a campus family, but feel a tie to the town of St. Johnsbury. Our students are well-known at local businesses, many within walking distance to campus, and countless friendships have formed and endured between day and boarding students. Overall, boarding at SJA offers a rich tapestry of support, structure, independence, and global community that shapes students into compassionate, engaged young adults.

> *St. Johnsbury Academy prepared me exceptionally well for college – both academically and socially. I took AP and college preparatory classes, while also exploring electives in the arts and career and technical education. I lived in the dorms with students from around the world, many of whom spoke different languages and introduced us to a wide range of cultures. At one point, it was said that our student body spoke over 15 different languages. Where else can you find an experience like that? You can – at St. Johnsbury Academy.*
>
> – Anna '23

Alumni – mentors and benefactors

SJA has over 13,000 alumni who have representation all over the world. Just a few of our most notable and historic alumni include:

- Charles Hosmer Morse, 1850, Founder of Fairbanks-Morse Corporation
- Linda Richards, 1859, America's first trained nurse
- Wallace Abbott, 1882, Founder of Abbott Laboratories,
- Caroline S. Woodruff, 1884, first woman President of Castleton University
- Calvin Coolidge, 1891, 30th US president from 1923–1929

- Benjamin T. Marshall, 1893, President of Connecticut College
- Dr. Bob Smith, 1898, Founder of AA (Alcoholics Anonymous)

Alumni play a vital role in supporting current students, helping to strengthen the fabric of the institution in meaningful and lasting ways. Through generous financial contributions, alumni help fund scholarships, academic programs, campus improvements, and extracurricular opportunities that directly benefit students. Beyond financial support, many alumni return to campus to share their experiences, offer career insights, and participate in panels or classroom discussions, enriching the learning environment and inspiring the next generation.

Alumni also serve as valuable mentors, providing guidance to students navigating academic and professional paths. Their networks often open doors for internships, college admissions, or job opportunities, giving students a strong head start as they enter the next stage of their lives. This ongoing involvement helps maintain a supportive community that bridges generations and keeps the spirit and success of the institution alive.

> *While earning my master's degree was a significant achievement, it is the connections I built at St. Johnsbury Academy that have proven most impactful in my professional journey. The mentorship and support from fellow alumni not only guided me through key decisions but also played a direct role in helping me secure an internship during my undergraduate degree and then connected me with professionals that helped me land a job and relocate to a major city within weeks of graduating with my master's.*

Their influence has far exceeded what I gained from either of my colleges.

– Jacob '19

Summary

St. Johnsbury Academy's uniqueness lies in our combined breadth and depth: a comprehensive curriculum, specialized signature paths, expert faculty, and reflective traditions that foster character, inquiry, and community. Whether through daily Chapel, senior Capstones, global exchanges, or community service, SJA lives its motto: *Semper Discens* – Always Learning. What emerges is not just preparation for post-secondary life, but transformation into competent, compassionate citizens ready to shape a better world – true to its founding vision and ever-evolving promises.

Addendum

During the time this book was being published, St. Johnsbury Academy was embarking on a community project to review the mission and core values of the institution to ensure they reflect the school's commitments in the 21st century. Although not yet finalized, the drafted materials build upon the strong foundation of our current mission – to challenge our students to be deep thinkers, bold creators, and responsible members of society – and further ground us in the values of optimism, connection, opportunity and innovation.

Kimball Union Academy

Location: Meriden, New Hampshire

Year Founded: 1813

Grades Served: 9–12 + Post Grad

Total Enrollment: 340

Percent Boarding: 77%

Percent Non-White: 40%

Percent From Out of State: 79%

Percent From Out of Country: 24%

2025–26 School Year Tuition: $80,100

Percent Who Receive Financial Aid: 34%

School Website: www.kua.org

Head of School: Tyler Lewis

Kimball Union Academy

Chapter Completed By
Tyler Lewis, Head of School

A Place of Purpose

In the early 1800s, Kimball Union was one of a small handful of boarding schools in the United States. The original benefactor, Daniel Kimball made his fortune in the "wool boom" of the late 1700s, a period of New England's history that is still visible today in the campus' pastoral setting scattered with hand-built stone walls. Like so many schools of that time, our original charter distinctly states that KUA was a school for the education of young men, yet, all records and class photos you will see around campus clearly show that our school was not only coeducational but a community of many races. In our earliest year, KUA was breaking its own rules to embrace diversity. We were not only well ahead of our time among boarding schools, but also among the great higher education neighbors of our region. The first female graduate of Middlebury College and Dartmouth College's first Native and non-white students were graduates of Kimball Union Academy before trailblazing access at the collegiate level.

Our histories not only tell us so much about where we came from and the foundational values that brought our Academy to life, but they also provide an enduring strength and depth to our identity. As we chart our path forward, we know KUA proudly opened its doors to international students alongside students from throughout New England and launched generations of affirming practices that continue to guide the school today.

We are situated in the intellectual and cultural umbrella that spreads out from our neighbors, Dartmouth College, and we also sit in the fertile Connecticut River Valley nestled between the peaks of the Appalachian Mountains. Walking across campus inspires awe and appreciation for the beauty of our natural surroundings that puts curious minds only inches away from ponderings on sustainability and our role in preserving the amazing natural resources and landscapes that are so present in our daily rhythm. Visitors making their first trip to our campus are stopped in their tracks and fumbling for their cameras as they capture selfies of the magnificent views that are the backdrop to life on campus. Whether it is your inclination to explore the peaks of the surrounding mountains or take in the view from right here on campus, the beauty and calm nature makes an ideal setting for learning and building meaningful relationships.

A proud history of inclusion and an authentic connection to place are two hallmarks of Kimball Union. Our history finds us "standing there waiting" when these topics cyclically rise to the consciousness of individuals or society. Today we draw our inspiration from those who walked these grounds before us and yet never rest on the belief that the world will cease to change. We empower our students to rise to the challenges of the day by educating and supporting them to lead in areas such as technology and industry, mental health and wellbeing, character, sustainability, and climate.

> *KUA is animated by our history and through our landscape. We each experience it differently, but collectively, we are*

blessed with amazing environmental resources, cultural opportunities, and jaw-dropping beauty.

– Blaine Kopp, EE Just Chair of Environmental Science

A School with a Soul

A foundational commitment to knowing and to understanding each individual in our community is not only central to our mission, but also evident in the culture that develops each year on our campus. We think deeply about not only the words that we choose but their depth of meaning and the commitment they compel upon us to deliver. Our mission statement stands out as unique and it calls to people who are searching for a school with a soul.

We are a community committed to values and to an experience that will seek out and honor the unique individual at the core of each and every community member. We start with "belonging" as the fundamental work for everything we do. For generations KUA has prioritized the importance of each member of the community feeling safe, appreciated for who they are as a person, and valued for their unique skills and characteristics. We believe this is rooted in the same instincts that drive great parenting – healthy relationships creating an environment for our children to lean into and trust that they are known and appreciated for who they are – and that they can leverage that support into confidence to expand their comfort zones and take social and intellectual risks that will exponentially accelerate their learning.

Over the past few decades there have been evolutions in education that have affirmed many of the instincts that have been foundational to education and, in fact, dispelled others. As neuroscience has deepened our evidence-based understanding of how we learn, it has captured our full attention and refined the ways that we teach. Kimball Union has transformed a high-functioning learning center into a center for teaching and learning that relies on evidence-based research that has revolutionized our approach by clarifying the practices that are most effective in every learner. We now embrace a philosophy – KUA Design – that we apply across every educational experience. It provides a science-informed framework for educators to guide their professional development and engagement with students so they can deliver what every student deserves – the best possible learning environment for holistic adolescent growth.

> *Waking up every morning excited to go to classes was a feeling I had never experienced before. Seeing my friends every morning and learning new material was very refreshing in an environment that felt safe and friendly.*
>
> – Kai '25

We know that engagement lies at the heart of deep learning – images of the brain inform some of our very best instincts and show that when engagement is maximized, we are at our peak opportunity for learning. Understanding that fact drives a push for nurturing curiosity, experiential learning, connection to global themes and relevant topics and the most impactful of all – a personal connection. As a result, we are called upon to provide a sense of belonging in the learning environment. The science of learning affirms the art of teaching and that has only accelerated our resolve to ask, what else should we ensure is a part of every student experience?

One answer is a multitude of opportunities and pathways for explorations that support growth and development, and those are evident all throughout our academic and co-curricular programs. Modern education needs to be aware of and adjusting to the evolution that is occurring in the skills and talents that will be essential in a world that is fundamentally a human experience, yet increasingly technologically advanced. Knowledge, skills, and character remain central building blocks of education, but some of the targeted skills and knowledge are evolving. Where KUA Design, our educational philosophy, guides how we teach, what we teach is also critically important to ensuring we prepare this generation of learners for the needs of their life and time.

Our students are encouraged throughout their journey to explore more deeply the areas of curiosity for them – to deepen their engagement by pursuing courses that align with their interest and even to pursue a track toward one of our Scholar Programs. With endowments that support research, travel, and personal exploration, we offer programs for interests in Global, Arts or STEM themes to enrich the student experience by focusing additional coursework, along with visiting lectures, school-sponsored travel, and the opportunity to unravel an area of particular interest through a culminating senior thesis.

One of the most influential ways our students are exposed to the vast opportunities the world can offer them is through the relationships they develop with their peers. One in five KUA students come from countries outside the United States, creating a richer, deeper high-school experience. Growing up in a community through shared living and learning spaces where both guided and unscripted conversations draw out relationships and perspectives, makes the world feel smaller and more familiar for all.

We also expose our students to new perspectives by working with other schools that embrace our values and philosophies. We are fortunate to be the only North American school that is part of an eight school collaboration, the Global Alliance for Innovative Learning (GAIL). The other GAIL Schools, located in Australia, Peru, India, South Africa, New Zealand, Scotland and China are also looking to the future to prepare leaders with a commitment to understanding and to embracing their place in a global community. An annual conference hosted by one of the schools brings students, teachers, and administrators together to discuss themes we bring back to our community and are woven into our academic program. The past three years focused on leadership, sustainability, and diversity, and resulted in environmental pledges, multicultural offerings, student exchanges, visiting faculty and sustained dialogues and relationships among our students.

The interests of our students are increasingly related to the existential challenges that we see emerging on our planet. Data conclusively demonstrates that struggling to find hope is at the core of the decline in empathy and increased anxiousness of this generation – students are looking for understanding and a way to contribute to positive change. Being able to interpret media, and finding hope in sustainable food systems, energy alternatives, and carbon reduction to sustain our planet increasingly rise to the fore when students are working on topics of impact. We, in turn, pivot our attention to these topics in our curriculum. In addition to improving their skills on collaboration, critical thinking, resilience, and active listening we are taking deep dives into topics driving the global economy with global economics, sustainability and AI leading the charge.

We return to our philosophy of using science-informed research to guide our practices. For AI, that means looking holistically at its impact on the present and future educational needs for this generation of learners. Our Center for Sustainability not only provides deeply meaningful opportunities for hands-on learning, but we are also developing courses in collaboration with Dartmouth College and the Irving Institute for Energy and Society to have our students on the front edge of meaningful discussions and hopeful solutions. We are committed to inspiring solutions focused leaders for the topics our students are most drawn to impacting our modern world.

We are united by a shared curiosity and a drive to seek a better future. While our reasons for coming here may vary, our journeys have converged in this shared experience. Together we've created a community built on mutual support, shared growth, and collective purpose.

– Wisdom '26

Finding the Joy in Learning

Maximizing curiosity and engagement is a different journey for every student, so providing exposure to a broad range of experiences and challenges is an essential part of every KUA experience.

We believe that the safety net that our students feel through our investment in their sense of belonging empowers them to take more positive risks and explore new and unknown opportunities with increased confidence. At the same time, we want our students to understand that finding joy in learning will inspire their life journey well into the future. If they approach new opportunities and perspectives with enthusiasm, so much more of the world will open to them. By feeling safe, empowered, and encouraged to take the leap – our students develop habits to expand themselves in ways that lead to richer lives.

For many of our students the reward of committing to physical development through competition compels them to the exceptional coaching and training they can find in our athletics department. Each year, forty percent of our graduates go on to play a collegiate sport and one hundred percent of our students wear a KUA uniform at some point in their KUA career. The performing and/or studio arts are also a part of every student's journey and not only thrive at KUA but are the siren that calls many to our door. With an arts program as robust as any offering in the school, we craft a schedule that ensures our artists and athletes can thrive in both arenas without having to compromise on either. It's not uncommon to see a soccer player arriving for theater rehearsal after coming off the field – embracing all sides of their identity.

For other dimensions of our desire to engage, we offer unique opportunities for authentic and meaningful service including the only (as far as we are aware!) independent school student fire brigade in the country. The endowed program – born out of a student seeking to make amends for a lapse in judgement– puts students shoulder-to-shoulder with the town's volunteer firefighters in real-life situations that transform their world view, sense of responsibility and connection to community. A robust farm program, with roots in wartime food production, is embedded in our Center for Sustainability where the greenhouse is a hub for course offerings on decarbonizing your life and environmental science, as well as a thriving farm-to-table food production. The cycle of food waste feeding our pigs and our garden produce landing on our salad bar, to the tending of bees, chickens, and sheep are familiar to some of our students and a brand-new experience to our kids from the world's most populated cities. Each spring, the opportunity to tap into maple trees and boil sap in our hand-built timber-framed sugar house serves as a point of pride in our sense of place.

All these experiences, and the plethora of others we offer, including those our students create, help feed curiosity and inspire learning. By ensuring that every KUA student wears a uniform in competition, finds themself on stage performing or creating in the studio, participates in service to the direct benefit of others, and engages with sustainability topics, we light a spark that continues to shine as their definition of 'self' is irreversibly expanded.

Supporting the Whole Student

None of our exceptional programming would have meaning if we didn't provide an anchor of wellbeing rooted in the trust that they are surrounded by people prioritizing them feeling safe, connected, and appreciated for who they are becoming as a person. A peek behind the curtain would reveal an intricately woven network of adults – teachers, coaches, counselors, advisors, dorm parents – constantly in conversation to ensure every student is having a healthy academic and social-emotional experience. As time goes on, we observe students practicing self-advocacy and identifying and utilizing practices that demonstrate they understand and value the importance of a balanced life. We not only model and provide many examples and pathways for securing a foundation of wellbeing, but our students also create opportunities and invite others to participate. In the past year, polar plunge, yoga, meditation, cooking, affinity groups, and a running club all emerged from students inviting others to join them in these spaces. Loneliness is identified as a public health concern with young adults measuring some of the highest rates. We talk with our students about moving through life with interests and with community and an awareness of how to stay connected, active and engaged.

> *These wonderful people make you feel welcomed and valued. I feel like since I have been here, I am not just learning at a school, I am also growing as an individual and discovering so much more about myself and my potential that I never knew.*
>
> – Nasean '27

From their earliest days on campus, our students are asked to create a campus-wide sense of belonging by realizing that it is not our right, but rather our responsibility to create a space for all others to join in community. In focusing on creating the space for others to feel connected, we know that it is, in turn, gifted back to us with exponential returns. When both adults and students approach one another with a sense of humanity, appreciation and care a community develops where everyone feels appreciated for being – just who they are. It takes time and patience, but when it works, there's nothing better than seeing teenagers discover the rewarding feeling of their own positive actions.

Of course, philosophies are strengthened and clarified through programming. Our four-year students begin their career in an intentionally designed ninth-grade program we call Nine by Design. A ninth-grade team, supported by adults focused on residential and advising duties, meets weekly to guide the class forward through programming that targets empathy and kindness, identity, and self-care, as well as foundational academic skills. An extra layer of support at the edges of every experience helps them to see around corners and minimize the anxiety associated with being new or having to "sink or swim." We know that the first year of high school has an outsized impact on a student's graduation and is a critical time for students to develop a positive perception of themselves as learners. We've seen this model for holistic support translate into grounded, successful students and a near 100 percent retention rate.

Part of our approach to wellbeing is considering areas where students can feel marginalized or where the philosophies and ideals of our community might collide with other preexisting norms. At KUA, we compete in athletics at the highest level in every season and are proud of the dedication and the success that our teams achieve through their commitment to one another, their coaches, and their progress. We recognize how meaningful athletics is to the identity and joy of our students and we want to cultivate an inclusive community free from harassment of any kind as individuals and teams compete in athletic pursuits. Therefore, we ensure that the same values we uphold in our classrooms, residence halls, and dining hall are consistent with what happens in interscholastic competitions.

We recently adopted a STAND Up to Harassment policy for all our interscholastic sports and have asked the schools of the Lakes Region League to join us, which was recently adopted in our league-wide code of conduct. It simply states our intolerance for gender-based, race-based, or other forms of hate speech in our competitions and outlines protocols that support players, coaches, and officials to take immediate action in the case of an incident. Our belief in the clarity of these guidelines illuminates that adrenaline in competition is not an excuse for hate and it has had an immediate impact on actions and elevated the safety and wellbeing of our student-athletes, as well as our opponents. We are encouraging adoption of this policy by the governing body of New England Prep School athletics knowing that leading with our values is central to the feeling of safety for all.

At KUA, we approach our work with the humility to realize that there are both timeless elements to our work, as well as pieces needing persistent connection to the changing world. Throughout our literature, we note that we are steeped in history, yet unbound by tradition. So, as we walk with our students through the teenage years that have always been synonymous with some of the most dynamic and transformative changes – physically, neurologically, intellectually, hormonally and emotionally. We acknowledge this generation is coming of age at a time of rapid change in technology, the environment, global relations, and human connections. Our students are aware of these changes, inextricably connected to them, and our approach to education prioritizes an understanding and appreciation for all that teens are experiencing – both internally and in their external environment. At the very core of our community are the values that not only opened our doors, but created a place of belonging for a mix of genders and races dating back to the early 1800s. What science now affirms, we have practiced for generations, as our hearts and our minds come together in knowing that everything we build must rise up from a foundation of being seen, known and appreciated for who each of us is, as an individual. Holistic growth starts from being seen and then layering in experiences and challenges in an awe-inspiring environment, to elevate these years to the most fulfilling, exciting, and engaging journey we can imagine. We hope to see you soon on The Hilltop.

Gould Academy

Location: Bethel, Maine

Year Founded: 1836

Grades Served: 9–12 + Post Grad

Total Enrollment: 220

Percent Boarding: 70%

Percent Non-White: 20%

Percent From Out of State: 53%

Percent From Out of Country: 20%

2025–26 School Year Tuition: $75,324

Percent Who Receive Financial Aid: 40%

School Website: www.gouldacademy.org

Head of School: Tao Smith

Gould Academy

Chapter Completed By

Tao Smith, Head of School

Prepared for the Moment That Matters

It is the middle of July, and the heat hangs heavy. I am standing in the parking lot of a small community hospital in western Maine with my colleague's wife and daughter, watching a helicopter descend while we wait for an ambulance to arrive. We do not yet know if Dave is alive or dead. All we know is that a sheriff's deputy used his phone to call and say there had been a bike accident and that we should come quickly.

Dave is not only a trusted colleague of more than fifteen years. He is family and a godparent to one of my children. As the helicopter circles lower, the ordinary details of our shared life – workdays, conversations, rituals – feel suddenly fragile and suspended.

We arrived before the ambulance. Later, we would learn what had happened. A volunteer firefighter happened upon the scene by chance. He recognized Dave immediately and knew his medical history. When he reached him, there was no pulse. No breath. Quick action and practiced CPR brought him back – broken ribs, but a beating heart – long enough for emergency responders to stabilize him and transport him here.

As we waited, time stretched and collapsed all at once. We did not know how long he had been without oxygen, what damage might already have been done, or what would come next. We knew almost nothing.

In moments like these, the mind searches for something familiar – something steady to hold onto when nothing feels certain. That grounding arrived in the form of a recent Gould Academy graduate, now serving as an emergency medical technician.

In this moment, she was not a former student but a familiar and trusted authority. While her team prepared to transfer Dave from the ambulance to the helicopter, Sophia came straight toward us. She told us he was alive, though unconscious. She explained that his heart had stopped seven times on the way to the hospital. He was stable now. Did we want to say goodbye before they loaded him onto the helicopter?

I burst into tears. Sophia wrapped her arms around me, then around Kathleen, steady and sure. For the first time in over an hour, I took a breath. Sophia was not acting as a former student. She was acting as a young adult who had been trusted, trained, challenged, and supported – again and again – by a school designed to do exactly that.

Where Place Teaches

What distinguishes Gould is not simply its location, but the expectations that come with it: attention, effort, reflection, and responsibility. These are habits learned slowly, shaped by daily practice and reinforced over time by both the people and the place itself.

Set back from the pace that defines much of adolescent life, Bethel offers something increasingly rare: space. Not the absence of structure, but room – room to slow down, to notice, to remain with an idea or a challenge long enough for it to matter. For students arriving from crowded schedules and lives of constant motion, this small Maine town in the foothills of the White Mountain National Forest becomes a kind of pause. Growth here is shaped as much by landscape and community as by lessons and experiences;

mentors are present not only in formal settings, but in the ordinary, unscripted moments when learning most often takes hold.

This understanding of place as integral to education has been present from the school's beginning. In 1835, Dr. Nathaniel Tuckerman True opened a school on Bethel Hill that would later become Gould Academy. True believed learning should extend beyond classroom walls and into lived experience. He took students into the surrounding fields and woods not as a break from study, but as an extension of it – trusting that curiosity, confidence, and character develop through direct engagement with the world. As recorded in the Museums of the Bethel Historical Society Online Collections and Catalogue, Dr. True instructed his students:

> *not only in theory but in practice, and it was his delight to take his spring and summer classes in botany through the fields, pastures and woods, gathering and classifying the various wild flowers in their season, or his pupils interested in mineralogy and geology to the summit of Paradise Hill, and sometimes even to the tops of surrounding mountains...*

That belief remains visible today, especially in winter. Each morning begins outdoors, as students travel from Gould's village campus to the mountain campus at Sunday River Ski Resort. The routine is quiet and, at first glance, unremarkable. Over time, however, it builds something durable. Students learn to prepare – to gather what they need, to read conditions, to take responsibility for showing up ready.

Whether they are clicking into race skis and snowboards, training as Ski Patrollers, teaching local elementary students, or navigating unfamiliar backcountry terrain, they learn to take responsibility for their gear, their decisions, and the people around them. They learn to listen to feedback, adjust, and try again. Between runs, in conversations that aren't scheduled or scripted, students begin to imagine who they might become if they keep practicing this kind of attention.

This rhythm is intentional, though it rarely announces itself as such. From the beginning, Gould understood the surrounding landscape not as scenery but as a teacher, and learning not as something confined to a period or a classroom, but as something shaped by repetition, relationship, and trust.

At Gould, time in nature is not a reward. It is part of the work. A daily practice in presence and responsibility, shared across disciplines and experience levels. The confidence that grows there doesn't stay in the mountains. It carries back into classrooms: sustained inquiry, reflection, revision, and intellectual risk-taking serve students well in demanding college environments, as well as on the mountain and in athletic competitions.

Students are not shaped by accident here. They are shaped slowly, through attention and responsibility, in a place designed to give them the space and guidance to grow into lives of fulfillment and purpose.

Building Resilience: The Legacy of True, Gehring, and Clough

Dr. John George Gehring (1857–1932) brought to Bethel a vision of wellness that was both expansive and deeply human. In his Bethel clinic, Dr. Gehring dedicated 35 years to serving patients from around the world. His work rested on a simple but demanding premise: that lasting health requires attention to the whole person.

Gehring encouraged patients to understand themselves as integrated beings, writing that "man is neither wholly an animal, an intelligence or a spirit, but all three, and he cannot hope to maintain his balance unless all three legs of the tripod which comprise his whole are recognized and used."

His approach – attentive to body, mind, and spirit, and grounded in reflection and narrative – feels strikingly modern.

This philosophy found expression not only in words but also in daily practice. Physical activity was central to Gehring's therapeutic vision; patients were encouraged – sometimes insistently – to chop wood, garden, snowshoe, hike, and play tennis. As documented in the Museums of the Bethel Historical Society Online Collection and Catalogue, "movement and labor were understood not as distractions from healing, but as essential to it." Over time, these ideas helped shape the cultural soil of Bethel itself, and Gould, where Gehring was a trustee and married to Dr. Tuckerman True's daughter, Marian True Farnsworth.

Gould's unofficial motto, "To Thine Own Self Be True," is often traced to this same way of thinking – a belief that self-knowledge, effort, and reflection are inseparable from growth. That thread would re-emerge with particular clarity nearly a century later.

When Bill Clough became Gould's headmaster in 1983, he arrived with an instinctive understanding of education as a whole-person endeavor. Raised on a hilltop farm in New London, New Hampshire, Bill grew up immersed in the land – tending sheep, working with his mother's Connemara horses, hunting, and sugaring. Like Gould's early leaders, Dr. True and Dr. Gehring, he believed that education should shape the whole person, not just the mind. In searching for a school that prized curiosity, effort, and authentic joy over rigid rules or formulas, Bill and his wife, Ki, found Gould.

Bill brought intellect, athleticism, creativity, and care for students into every part of campus life. Like Gehring, Clough was known for early-morning excursions into the woods, accompanied by reluctant students, armed with splitting mauls, an axe, a chainsaw, and an old pickup truck, to fell, buck, and split firewood for the school's woodstoves and fireplaces.

There were few words spoken – just shared work, guidance in silence, and a quiet insistence that effort mattered. In these moments, students learned that adults could walk alongside them, offering trust, support, and challenge in equal measure.

Clough's philosophy had deep roots. In 1960, he participated in a six-month Outward Bound wilderness expedition that showed him the transformative power of deliberate challenge in the outdoors. In 1984, he brought that vision to Gould, creating the first 10-day winter expedition for juniors, which became the genesis of the Four Point Program: a curriculum of real-world challenge, reflection, and growth.

Programs like Four Point give structure to growth. Students encounter difficulty with guidance and support as they learn to navigate hard terrain, diverse cultures, community engagement, the joy and challenge of the arts, and sometimes the harder truths about themselves. Risk is embraced. Failure is expected. What matters is how students are supported when it happens. Part of the Four Point ritual is to give each student a paracord bracelet tied with slip knots upon course completion. A recent graduate reflects, "Looking at my Junior Four Point bracelet, it reminds me not only of my accomplishments but also that I have the ability to do difficult things based on what I have control over in the present."

At Gould, faculty are champions of students not by directing their paths, but by walking alongside them. As teachers, coaches, advisors, and dorm parents, they share their experience, passions, and care while paying close attention to who each student is becoming. Over time, their steady presence and intentional programming provide young people the confidence to take risks, reflect honestly, and begin to discover their purpose. Students are not pushed toward a single definition of success; they are supported as they grow into resilient, capable, and thoughtful adults – ready to engage the world with courage and care. This quiet, relational work is the heart of Gould's Portrait of a Graduate.

Gould's Portrait of a Graduate reflects a philosophy that has guided the school for nearly two centuries. Nathaniel Tuckerman True, Dr. Gehring, and Bill Clough each shaped a shared understanding of education as something lived as well as studied. From True came the belief that learning is deepest when students engage directly with the world beyond the classroom. Gehring emphasized the role of physical challenge, reflection, and adult mentorship in shaping character and judgment. Clough carried these ideas forward, designing programs like Four Point that ask students to meet real challenges with effort, awareness, and support.

That same philosophy guides Gould's academic life. In classrooms, students are invited to wrestle with ideas as seriously as they do with experience – through sustained inquiry, discussion, revision, and reflection. Faculty design courses that value curiosity and persistence, where original thinking is expected, and intellectual risk is encouraged. Together, academic and experiential learning form a single developmental arc, aligning place, program, and people to cultivate the whole adolescent – thoughtful, resilient, and prepared to engage the world with purpose.

That commitment takes its clearest shape in the Four Point Program.

Four Point: The Arc of Becoming

Four Point is Gould's signature experiential program – a four-year journey that engages students in ways the classroom alone cannot. Each March, students step away from traditional schedules and into transformational experiences that their interdisciplinary courses have prepared them for. International immersion, creative exploration, winter expeditions, and independent capstone projects invite students to reflect, connect, and test themselves in meaningful ways.

The program is intentionally designed to support holistic adolescent growth – social, emotional, intellectual, and physical – within a community where roles blur in important ways. The teacher who was guiding an AP Physics class weeks earlier may now be standing beside a student in snowshoes, navigating by map and compass. In these moments, learning becomes lived, and mentorship becomes visible.

Four Point: From Invention to Collaboration

Eli arrived at his senior Four Point project through years of coursework and questions that wouldn't let go. A tenth-grade observation – warmer water temperatures and more regular, intense rainstorms were threatening brook trout in a local river – turned into a research question that consumed him. By junior year, he was experimenting with homemade water sensors. His first attempts failed: data collected without timestamps, sensors zip-tied to bricks. But each iteration taught him more.

When senior Four Point arrived, Eli proposed designing affordable temperature-monitoring stations to help protect Maine's vulnerable trout habitat. IDEAS Center Director Billy Ayotte learned to code climate models alongside Eli and mentored him through prototype development.

Eli's final project demonstrated rigorous data analysis, environmental engineering, and policy argumentation at the State House. Yet the deeper growth was intellectual: Eli's thinking evolved from "my invention will solve this" to an understanding that collaboration, patience, and consensus-building are essential to any lasting solution. These are skills learned in the quiet moments of mentorship across all disciplines – the ability to listen, to revise thinking, to see problems as part of larger systems. Four Point gave Eli the structure to pursue a question over multiple years and the expectation that his work could contribute meaningfully. He now studies environmental science and policy at a leading liberal arts college, carrying forward the understanding that technical skill matters, but so does the capacity to work alongside others toward solutions that endure.

Four Point: Mentorship Across Disciplines

Junchao arrived at Gould as a one-year experiment – a talented alpine ski racer from Maryland seeking space to foster his intellectual curiosity. For Junchao, that space lay within Four Point's framework for exploration. Through art and design coursework, he developed technical skills in blacksmithing and woodworking. Summer internships in architecture and real estate shifted his thinking from "I enjoy making things" to an understanding of how creativity serves larger systems – market realities, strategy, and decision-making. Art teacher Kipp Greene pushed him to make work more complex and intentional. College counselor Maggie Davis helped him connect experiences to purpose.

The quiet support of mentors across disciplines made his growth possible. His ski coaches, recognizing his deepening commitment to architecture, encouraged him to pursue that passion fully – understanding that athletic excellence and intellectual development need not compete but can reinforce one another. By senior year, Junchao's architecture program portfolio demonstrated not just artistic talent but disciplined, systems-level thinking. His highly selective college acceptance reflected years of sustained inquiry: craft learned through patient mentorship, analytical thinking developed in coursework, and professional maturity gained through internships.

Gould's Four Point provided Junchao structure to turn interest into direction, even when it meant stepping away from what others might have expected.

Four Point: From Advocate to EMT

Sophia, whom we last met offering comfort to her former Head of School, provides a living example of this philosophy – from self-discovery to moments demanding real-world courage. Sophia has continued her work as an EMT, and often sees Dave in the community. They share a bond that transcends words.

Sophia's freshman year began with frustration when COVID canceled the Four Point international trip, but her English teacher supported her creativity and courage by encouraging her to speak up. "This needs to be your fight," he told her. With guidance, Sophia drafted a proposal, discovering her voice and agency – skills essential to later academic and leadership work. Sophomore year shifted outward as service and art projects taught her to navigate group dynamics. Junior year brought the winter expedition, where the hardest lessons were not the demanding physical exertion, but the social and emotional hurdles – learning to trust adults as guides and rely on peers. "I went into the woods a kid and came back a grown-up," she reflects. By senior year, experiences converged with academic rigor. As a Ski Patroller, Sophia passed demanding written exams and practical assessments. Her capstone – a six-week EMT course alongside pre-med students in college – required mastering complex medical knowledge and passing a rigorous certification exam. Initially intimidated, she drew on resilience honed through Four Point and analytical discipline from coursework. Weeks after graduating from Gould, practicing as a fully certified first responder, she was no longer a student but a trusted adult whose competence emerged through the intentional interweaving of intellectual challenge, experiential learning, and relentless support.

These stories demonstrate what Four Point makes possible: curiosity, creativity, courage, and designed risk-taking within a network of support, and programs that cultivate the whole adolescent – intellectually, emotionally, physically, and socially. Academic rigor and experiential challenge are interwoven threads of the same developmental arc. A student wrestling with complex questions in a seminar builds the same analytical courage needed to navigate unfamiliar terrain. The creative risk required to revise a thesis mirrors the vulnerability of stepping into leadership. Here, the influence of True, Gehring, and Clough endures: place, program, and people aligned to help young adults emerge not only resilient and thoughtful, but intellectually rigorous and analytically capable – ready to live with courage, purpose, and the skills to engage a complex world.

Trusted Adults: Mentorship as the Multiplier

Gould does not guarantee student success. It promises mentorship. And it begins with who we hire. Teachers, coaches, and dorm parents are selected not only for content knowledge or technical skill, but for their capacity to know students deeply, to recognize when to push and when to pause, and to guide growth through relationship. These adults are trained in adolescent development and coached to see learning as iterative and human, shaped as much by trust as by challenge.

At Gould, mentors create conditions where students are invited to extend themselves beyond what feels comfortable – whether that means winter camping for nine days, stepping into leadership on Ski Patrol, or navigating complex group dynamics far from familiar support systems. Just as importantly, those same adults stay close over time. They scaffold growth through repeated experiences, reflection, and feedback, helping students make meaning of challenge rather than simply survive it. And when focus wavers – as it inevitably does in adolescence – mentors help students refine their attention, name what matters, and reclaim agency. Sophia, Eli, and Junchao's stories make this visible: teachers who insisted on advocacy, advisors who guided through social growth, mentors who entrusted them with real responsibility, and adults who stayed present long enough for confidence to turn into competence.

Learning happens everywhere. In classrooms. On mountains and fields and trails. In dorms, at dinner tables, on teams. And in those places, adults are learning too – watching carefully, adjusting, reflecting, growing alongside young people.

Held together by this place and these relationships – a network of trusted adults, intentionally chosen and prepared for this work – students are given more than the chance to succeed. They are given the space to grow: socially, emotionally, intellectually, and physically. Over time, that growth becomes who they are. These are the graduates Gould sends into the world.

Confidence, Carried Forward

Growing up at Gould rarely happens all at once. It unfolds in moments – some ordinary, some extraordinary – when a young person realizes they are capable of more than they once believed. It happens in a 24/7 boarding community, where learning does not end with the school day, and adults are present not in shifts, but in relationship. Teachers, coaches, and dorm parents live the work alongside students – sharing meals, late nights, early mornings, and the quiet accumulation of trust.

Gould does not promise a particular outcome or a scripted version of success. It promises challenge and presence: a rigorous interdisciplinary curriculum, an extraordinary mountain setting, and committed adults who know students well, who challenge them honestly, and who stay close long enough for confidence to take root. Over time, that continuity matters. It is what allows preparation to become instinct.

That is why, on a hot July afternoon in a hospital parking lot, when a helicopter's blades cut through the air and nothing felt certain, a young

EMT moved forward with calm authority. Sophia did not summon that steadiness out of nowhere. It was built – slowly, repeatedly – through years of being known, guided, and trusted in a community designed to walk with adolescents as they grow up. In that moment, Gould was present too, not as a place she once attended, but as a way of being she carried with her: grounded, capable, and ready to meet the world with care.

Mercersburg Academy

Location: Mercersburg, Pennsylvania

Year Founded: 1893

Grades Served: 9–12 + Post Grad

Total Enrollment: 440

Percent Boarding: 83%

Percent Non-White: 42%

Percent From Out of State: 73%

Percent From Out of Country: 22%

2025–26 School Year Tuition: $78,900

Percent Who Receive Financial Aid: 50%

School Website: www.mercersburg.edu

Head of School: Quentin McDowell

Mercersburg Academy

Chapter Completed By

Quentin McDowell, Head of School

"We are the best kept secret in boarding schools." Like a badge of honor, this was long the refrain of Mercersburg Academy. This stunningly beautiful school with a rich history and a storied heritage is just far enough off the beaten path that the frequency in which it is mentioned belies its true, transformative nature. For the many thousands of Mercersburg faithful, however, this is part of the school's magic; a place that offers all of the bells and whistles of the most highly regarded boarding schools in the nation, yet without the many sharp edges typical of its peer institutions.

It is largely because of its location that Mercersburg Academy is what it is today. Set in the rolling hills of south-central Pennsylvania, closer to Washington, DC (90 minutes) than to either Philadelphia or Pittsburgh, Mercersburg is neatly nestled inside a small and charming town of only 1,500 residents, surrounded by seemingly endless stretches of farmland. When famous American poet Carl Sandburg visited Mercersburg Academy in 1943, he remarked on its timeless quality by saying, "This is a place on which time has laid its hands." What Sandburg witnessed over 80 years ago remains true today. There is an enduring element to the school, originally designed to replicate the best of New England boarding school gravitas and prestige in the mid-Atlantic region. The distinct difference that emerged given the unique geography, and one that is now deeply rooted in the school's ethos, is what the founding headmaster and those who have carried on his legacy for well over a century call the Mercersburg Spirit.

Mercersburg opened its doors in the fall of 1893, led by Phillips Exeter Academy and Princeton University graduate, Dr. William Mann Irvine. The school's educational history dates to 1836, when the campus was home to Marshall College. In 1853, it moved to Lancaster, Pennsylvania and merged with Franklin College to form what is now Franklin & Marshall College. The boarding school that Mercersburg Academy is today was designed by Dr. Irvine to be the "Exeter of the West," reflecting the notion that central Pennsylvania, at least at one point, was seen as the beginning of the western frontier. What Dr. Irvine set in motion was truly remarkable. Since its founding more than 130 years ago, Mercersburg Academy has produced countless notable alumni, including two Academy Award winners, a former president of Ecuador, governors, three Medal of Honor recipients, a Nobel Prize winner, and more Olympians than any other American high school on record. First built on a dream and a mountain of debt, the school's endowment per student now ranks in the top ten of all U.S. boarding schools and the idyllic campus that began with only 4 acres of leased land currently stretches out over 300 acres in the beautiful and bucolic setting of rural Pennsylvania.

Although Dr. Irvine embarked on building an incomparable school in 1893, he instead planted the seed for what would become a truly sacred place that finds its real value not in the transactional nature of outcomes, but in the transformational power of the experience. Mercersburg Academy is, by any standard, a remarkable institution that distinguishes itself among the nation's boarding schools. Unlike most, however, it is driven by something much deeper and far more profound than a pursuit of renowned prominence or perceived prestige. There is something special, daresay unique, about Mercersburg that has kept the school anchored to its singular purpose for well over a century: the Mercersburg Spirit. The Mercersburg Spirit is hard to define, but it permeates across the campus and resonates with all who have trod its paths. It is, for lack of a better description, a type of egalitarian and democratic drive to pursue excellence while always remaining firmly grounded in character and service. Perhaps it is best summarized by some of the school's earliest students who over a century ago, when writing in the school's yearbook, the Karux, outlined foundational elements of Mercersburg Academy and its formidable spirit.

> *Lofty ideals, great faith, noble integrity, and a ceaseless devotion to a mighty task – these are among the things that account for the meaning of Mercersburg.*
>
> – 1918 Karux Editors

Now, over 100 years later, the Mercersburg Spirit remains alive and well. Mercersburg Academy is a school that still values merit over social status and cares most about the growth of the "whole student." For evidence of this at today's Mercersburg, look no further than the first line of the mission statement: "At Mercersburg Academy we embrace the values of hard work, character, and community while learning to balance independence with interdependence and individual humility with collective pride."

These values – hard work, character, and community – are particularly important now at a time of rapid change and increasing isolation. Mercersburg remains committed to helping students balance their own pursuits and interests (independence) with the reality that they will inevitably need to rely on others (interdependence) as they navigate a complex and demanding world. Finally, it is an institution that celebrates modesty and humility at an individual level along with possessing a pervasive sense of shared pride and loyalty amongst all who are connected to the school.

It is remarkable how consistently these values – this spirit – are evident in daily life at Mercersburg. You see it when the entire football team shows up at the winter musical to watch their starting quarterback sing on stage, bravely daring to be more than just an athlete. You see it when a group of seniors selflessly and enthusiastically celebrate the early decision college acceptance received by a peer when they just found out that same day that they themselves did not get the decision they were hoping for. You see it when one of the students draws a picture on her napkin for the dining hall staff every day for the better part of a year hoping to convey her immense gratitude for their daily efforts. You see it at that same lunch (where the students have gathered daily with faculty to share a family style meal since 1893) when students of all ages connect freely with one another without the constraints of typical social dynamics and hierarchies. You see it when hundreds of students who traveled hours in the freezing cold of winter to watch their soccer team lose in overtime in the state championship lock arms and sing them the alma mater as a way of showing that their love and support is not defined by a win, but instead by the joy of being a part of the journey. You see it everywhere and every day at Mercersburg Academy.

When you meet alumni from Mercersburg, they may not rush to tell you all about their boarding school. In fact, it would be unusual if they did, given the value that is placed on humility. When the topic does come up, however, be prepared for what has at times been described as a borderline cult-like affection. Alumni often describe Mercersburg as a place that "changed my life," a phrase repeated so often it has become something of a shared refrain. Given this depth of loyalty, it should come as little surprise that the two largest donors in the school's history, Gerry Lenfest '49 and Debbie Simon '74, were both two-year students who came to Mercersburg at critical points in their lives when they were feeling lost and in need of a place that would not just stimulate their minds, but a community that would care for the entirety of their well-being. Gerry, who passed in August of 2018, gave over $100 million dollars to Mercersburg and Debbie, still an active member of the school community, has committed over $140 million dollars, making her not just Mercersburg's largest donor, but the single greatest female donor in U.S. independent school history. When asked about their Mercersburg experiences, Debbie and Gerry take it one step further, both at various times having said that the school actually saved their lives, reflecting that no amount of money or time could ever adequately convey their profound appreciation for Mercersburg.

It is obviously exciting to highlight the stories of people like Debbie Simon '74 and Gerry Lenfest '49, as they are unusual in terms of what they have been able to do for the school they love. That being said, the impact Mercersburg had on them during their most formative years is not particularly unusual. Tales of a similar nature abound and echo throughout the entire alumni community.

For example, Nikki H. was the first in her family to attend boarding school. She was a strong student and a promising young swimmer who had simply outgrown her local school and club. Nikki chose Mercersburg in part because of proximity (it was only an hour away from her hometown in Maryland) and also in part because of the school's fabled swimming program that had produced many All Americans and Olympians. And although Nikki, and her close-knit family, certainly wanted to find a school that would help her develop in the pool, she was also looking for a place that would nurture her curious mind and embrace her enthusiastic personality. Nikki found all of that and more at Mercersburg.

During her time at school, Nikki embraced every opportunity and thrived in a comprehensive environment that always encouraged as well as supported her. Her own impact on the community was great and, among other things, she served as a Peer Group Leader for new ninth graders, wrote for the Mercersburg News, was an active member of her Class Council, held various leadership roles, and eventually went on to captain the swim team. Even though she emerged as an exemplary role model in her own right, over time Nikki found herself in fond admiration of a select group of her peers – those who came to Mercersburg through its partnership with the United States Naval Academy (USNA) Foundation. For each year a small number of applicants to the U.S.Naval Academy are chosen to take part in the USNA Foundation, a program that guarantees them admittance to the Naval Academy upon successful completion of a post-graduate year at one of the Foundation partner schools, which includes Mercersburg. Nikki, who had the fortune to swim alongside a number of Foundation students, soon found herself so inspired by their dedication and commitment to a greater cause that she began to share in their dream to attend the Naval Academy. And like with everything else, when she put her mind to something, Nikki made it happen.

While in her first year at the Naval Academy, an officer once stopped Nikki and demanded to know why she was always smiling. Trying to conceal her widening grin, Nikki replied with something along the lines of, "because I love it here, sir!" Quickly admonished and dismissed in the moment, Nikki never let anything dampen her spirits. Determined to fly, she graduated and became a Navy pilot, flying the MH-60R Seahawk. She completed multiple global deployments, leading teams on missions ranging from submarine hunting to maritime reconnaissance. Reaching the rank of Lieutenant Commander, Nikki is now married with children, living in San Diego, California and transitioning to the private sector after well over a decade of service to her country. Not surprisingly, she is still smiling.

There is also Gnim B. who arrived at Mercersburg after growing up in New York City. Gnim was born in Togo and raised in New York after his mother won the U.S. visa lottery. He became involved with the community-based organization that helped keep children off the streets by engaging them in soccer – a sport that resonated deeply with many of the West African youth the group served. It was there that Gnim met Tom D. who was in charge of helping high achieving student athletes from the club get out of the city to attend private schools in the region. Gnim admits that he had his mind set on a school in New England, but after visiting three or four other schools, he chose Mercersburg. According to a student interview conducted with him, when he was asked "why Mercersburg," Gnim stated plainly that "the moment I arrived, I felt it. Something clicked."

And click it did. Gnim, who started at the beginning of his 11th grade year, hit the ground running. In his two years at Mercersburg, Gnim threw himself into a community that made him feel safe enough to take risks and try new things. He learned how to swim, struggled but found love in wrestling and for the beloved Coach Jacklin '96, became the varsity soccer captain, was a Blue Key tour guide, was selected as a prefect in his dormitory, and learned ballet in a dance class that he never dreamed he would someday take. In a speech Gnim delivered to a group of trustees on campus, Gnim shared that "being the school that Mercersburg is, I know there is nothing I can't do here." In only a couple of short years, his life had already begun to transform.

After graduation, Gnim continued to stay closely connected to Mercersburg, using what the school refers to as its Long Blue Line to help him leverage connections to land his first work study job in college, as well as a five-summer internship at New York firm, where he worked in immigration law at one of the top firms in the country. Now, Gnim has his own law degree and is a practicing attorney in New York. When looking back at his fateful decision to attend Mercersburg Academy, he shared that "Mercersburg didn't just prepare me academically, it taught me how to be organized, how to lead, and how to believe I belonged in spaces I never thought I'd enter."

The truth is that residential learning environments like Mercersburg Academy are not just about school. Many secondary institutions do the academic side of things exceptionally well. That is certainly not to say that the academic programming at Mercersburg is not excellent. Rooted in the science of learning and focused on content, meaning, and mastery, Mercersburg's curriculum is cohesive, intentional, and demanding. But high expectations should always be accompanied by high levels of support. Exceptionally invested faculty and carefully designed systems of support ensure that learning, not just grades, remains the central focus. All faculty commit to "fostering diversity of thought and respectful discourse through objective presentation of information and concepts so that learners can think critically and nurture their intellectual autonomy." As educators, we agree to implement best practices in the science of learning, facilitate personal connections with material, cultivate emotional safety, encourage students to find purpose and develop autonomy, provide opportunities for iteration, and support students in the transfer of knowledge to novel and varied settings.

This is what learning should look like: a student-centered approach that is equal parts college prep and relevant skill-based practices that leverages trust and celebrates the fact that the right amount of struggle leads to real growth. Mercersburg is proud of its willingness to press the formal boundaries of education and to fight against the complacency of "how we have always done things." Our academics are indeed a differentiator, but what really differentiates us from other schools is what goes on beyond the classroom. Mercersburg is uniquely well positioned to deliver a holistic program that far exceeds academic excellence. It is as much, if not more, about all the many intentional and thoughtful learning opportunities that occur after the final bell of the day. It is the informal moments, the residential life programming, the lessons learned on the stage or athletic fields, and that which occurs in the "seams" of boarding school life.

When families come to tour and interview at Mercersburg, they are greeted in the admission office by an engaging visit coordinator, quickly followed by their assigned admission officer. It is the job of this team to help anyone who walks through the doors of Traylor Hall feel warmly welcomed. Typically, however, the most important encounter a prospective student and family will have that day is with their Blue Key student tour guide. The excitement these student volunteers have to meet a family considering Mercersburg is almost always palpable. The reason for this is that everyone at Mercersburg very deliberately chose to attend the school. Yet another highlight of the school's more remote location is that students rarely just end up at Mercersburg. They make a deliberate choice, and it is in that choice that the real benefit lies: students at Mercersburg want to be there. Thus, they are excited about their institution and consequently happy to share their experiences with those considering doing the same. This sentiment also extends to the adults. Given the geography, very few faculty members land at Mercersburg by accident or by circumstance. Rather, they make the conscious decision to live and learn alongside the 440 students they have the privilege to serve. It is a notable thing to be able to confidently say this about every teacher and student at a school, and not something Mercersburg takes for granted.

It is on the school tour that prospective students and their families almost always ask the same question of their tour guide – "what kind of student does well at Mercersburg?" The guide's response is usually some version of the same thing. Where many schools have an archetype that can be readily described, outlining who will surely fit in and who will not, the Mercersburg answer reflects something different. The student guide rarely describes the features of an ideal candidate, instead they often rely on a single note of caution that, unsurprisingly, once again reflects the Mercersburg Spirit. It typically sounds something like, "the only students who don't do well at Mercersburg are those who try to be something other than themselves." In their own way, they try to convey that the community at large, and especially the students themselves, place high value on authenticity, regardless of interests, passions, or personality. If you can drop pretenses and reveal a true version of yourself, you will find a place at Mercersburg. Add in the well-researched fact that the most influential people in the lives of adolescents are their peers and adults who are not their parents and it is hard to imagine a better place for a child to be.

Just imagine the power in living and learning in a residential school environment during adolescence (one of life's hardest stretches of time) and feeling safe enough to be an authentic version of yourself. Consider what it would be like to wake up each morning at an institution that embodies its mission and is rooted in a deep sense of humility in spite of the innumerable resources and opportunities waiting to greet you throughout your day. Surrounded by like-minded and motivated peers, along with present and caring adults, the students at Mercersburg Academy are the school's sole focus.

If those of us who are now parents are honest with ourselves about how we felt when we were expecting our children, it's likely that our most important wish was for them to grow up healthy and happy, whatever that might mean and in whatever form that might take. Fast forward to the first play dates or the first years of school when they started socializing and many of us began to wonder how they compared to their peers and considered how they might define and differentiate themselves. from the other children. We thought about our own lives and how hard we worked to get where we were. We began to create a mental map of how our children could surpass our successes, achieve something great, be someone others think is important, and reach a level of financial and social security at or beyond our own limits. If only they go to the right schools, get the best grades, attend the most prestigious college, and land a big job – that would be enough to ensure their health and happiness. Or would it? And at what cost?

Here is where we hope to upend the false notion that success and happiness are mutually exclusive. Mercersburg Academy, over the course of more than a century and a quarter, operates on the premise that rigor, excellence, and traditionally desirable outcomes do not have to be sacrificed in favor of having a happy, healthy, and balanced high school experience. Rather, these can and must coexist and the entire student – the interconnected social, relational, emotional, physical, psychological, and intellectual aspects of what makes us whole – can be well served and cared for in the same place, at the same time.

Every student in the world deserves to go to a school like Mercersburg Academy, but the reality is that only very few will ever have the chance. But for the roughly 440 students who get the immense privilege of attending each year, the goal is relatively simple. How can we help them become the best versions of themselves so that they can best go on to lead and serve the world?

Avon Old Farms School

Location: Avon, Connecticut

Year Founded: 1927

Grades Served: 9–12 + Post Grad

Total Enrollment: Boys, 400

Percent Boarding: 75%

Percent From Out of State: 50%

Percent From Out of Country: 14%

2025–26 School Year Tuition: $78,200

Percent Who Receive Financial Aid: 40%

School Website: www.avonoldfarms.com

Head of School: Jim Detora

Avon Old Farms School

Chapter Completed By

Jacqueline Keller, Director of Marketing and Communications

A Village for Boys: Inside the Brotherhood of Avon Old Farms

If it's happened once, it's happened a thousand times: a boy steps through an archway of hand-hewn brownstone, blue slate underfoot, and emerges within an English-Cotswold style village unsure of the world he's just entered. What once might have been a journey of trepidation becomes one of comfort and, eventually, pride. That transition happens as boys discover the brotherhood that is the lifeblood of our century-old, all-boys institution, carefully fostered through Avon's holistic approach and commitment to educating the whole boy.

Alumni young and old will tell you it's a brotherhood that lasts a lifetime. They'll tell you it's the small moments that made all the difference and forged bonds with their classmates. They'll tell you it was their roommate or their calculus teacher who saw them in a moment of doubt and provided the support and gentle push forward that mattered. The Avon brotherhood is a network more valuable than their college fraternity. And Avonians will always say there's nothing quite like returning to Avon Old Farms and walking through those archways that haven't changed since they first arrived, knowing they're forever a part of something greater than themselves.

In 2027, Avon Old Farms will celebrate its centennial. Over the years, while society has demanded advanced approaches and technology, the essence of what makes Avon Old Farms work so well remains unchanged, preserved by a brotherhood that endures. It's a timeless institution that has stood firm, leaned into its identity, and has always led with one question that ensures we stay on-mission: What's best for the boys?

We Are Avonians

Avon Old Farms School was founded in 1927 by Theodate Pope Riddle, a pioneering American architect and philanthropist. Theodate's vision for Avon Old Farms was rooted in her belief in the transformative power of education. She was inspired to build a school that would provide a holistic educational experience that emphasized not only academic excellence but also character, leadership, and physical development. It is often cited that she wrote in her journals that she would one day create "an indestructible school for boys" and ultimately began creating plans for the school in 1918 as a lasting tribute to her late father. From the materials she used to the physical layout of campus buildings, Avon Old Farms was indeed constructed specifically to foster a community of boys.

Theodate believed in educating the whole boy and preparing boys to become responsible and well-rounded citizens. Influenced by the educational philosophies of progressive educators who advocated for experiential learning and the development of critical thinking skills, Avon Old Farms School formally opened its doors in September of 1927 with forty-eight students, a seven-member faculty, and a provost. At the first faculty meeting, Theodate laid out some of her plans for the school, including a concept familiar to Avonians of any era – Avon would be a student-centered school that provides not only an excellent education but also life skills. They would live alongside their dorm heads, would break bread with them in the refectory, and engage in meaningful academic pursuits as partners.

A century later, while many of the details of daily life have changed, that same culture persists. Where many faltered, Avon stood strong as a pillar of single-sex education, leaning into our traditions as a way to survive. Avon has always pushed not only our students but also our faculty in the pursuit of truth and excellence. Through war, depression, and pandemic, Avon time and again turned inward to find the best path forward. As Head of School Jim Detora consistently vocalizes, whenever Avon has a decision to make, we forge ahead with the same answer: do whatever is best for the boys.

Aspirando et Perseverando

Central to Theodate Pope Riddle's vision that has endured the test of time was the cultivation of character and leadership. She believed that education should not only challenge the mind but also shape the values of integrity, responsibility, and hard work. This philosophy is captured in the school's motto that she coined in our Deed of Trust, *Aspirando et Perseverando* - "To Aspire and To Persevere." It calls Avonians to reach for their highest potential, like an eagle in flight, while also embracing the steady, diligent perseverance of a beaver – symbolized by our unique mythical mascot, the Winged Beaver.

Today, *Aspirando et Perseverando* defines what it means to be an Avonian. From the first day on campus, students learn to embrace long-standing traditions that teach them that being a Man of Avon is a holistic pursuit: striving to achieve, contributing meaningfully to a community, and persevering through challenges together. In the classroom, on the playing field, and in life, it's easy to define excellence: high grades, Scholastic Gold Keys, Ivy League admissions, attention from athletic recruiters. Perseverance is often what cements excellence, and as a community, Avonians rely on one another to push beyond the norm.

Theodate's pioneering vision and our enduring motto continue to guide the Avon experience: cultivating young men who aspire boldly, persevere relentlessly, and engage fully in a community committed to learning, character, and growth. It is this integration of tradition, ambition, and resilience that shapes not only exceptional scholars but also conscientious, capable, and principled leaders. This vision has formed a brotherhood that knows it can rely on itself, even years after boys spread their wings and soar beyond our village in the woods.

Several years ago, a student's parent was talking at an open house event, sharing what she had seen develop in her son over his time at Avon. She said, "An Avon education isn't about the next four years, it's about the next 40," expressing exactly what Avon hopes to achieve with our students. It was astonishing how poignant that sentence was, and we've heard student ambassadors repeating it on campus over the years.

R.E.A.L. Learning

Avon understands that inspiring future young leaders requires educating boys amid a changing landscape of education. We've always aimed to teach our students how to think critically, not tell them what to think. To accomplish this, Avon employs a system of R.E.A.L. Learning. The tenets of R.E.A.L. Learning – Relational, Experiential, Active, and Lifelong – inform not only how we educate boys but also why we educate boys.

Relational:

Students form strong, lasting relationships with teachers and peers through classroom interactions, dormitory life, extracurriculars, residential programs, and family-style meals. These connections are vital to the teaching and learning process.

Experiential:

Meaningful and lasting knowledge is gained through relevant experiences that extend classroom learning. From US History students reenacting the Civil War with a teacher in the Oak Grove to physics students learning about friction in the hockey rink, experiential learning is a core part of the Avon experience, fostering a personal connection to learning.

Active:

Recognizing that prolonged sitting hinders focus, especially for boys, Avon Old Farms encourages students to be physically active during class when appropriate. Beyond movement, students are expected to be active participants in their own education, taking ownership of their studies for a transformative, rather than transactional, learning experience.

Lifelong:

Avon aims to cultivate lifelong learners who understand that growth is continuous. Students are encouraged to be curious and find ways to learn and contribute meaningfully, leading purposeful and rewarding lives.
A significant part of R.E.A.L. Learning is ensuring that boys are given opportunities to learn from the experiences of others. Through our Morning Meetings, Compass Program, Chapel Talks, and more, Avon has dedicated time to character-building programs that we believe are the core of an Avon education. Our seniors give Chapel Talks to the entire

community twice a week, often sharing tales of heroism, vulnerability, hardship, or perseverance. Our faculty give Compass Talks, which serve as a space for faculty to share a personal story of how they've found direction in life, offer wisdom, and once more, build meaningful relationships with the students. Twice a week, students are broken into either grade-level seminars or small groups to engage in topics like leadership, personal growth, health and wellness, and more.

Additionally, Avon prides itself in building a community of strong character: we emphasize the need to walk around campus with your head up, making eye contact with those you pass and greeting each other genuinely. Our current head of school has even banned the use of cell phones in communal spaces and while walking around campus to emphasize the point of being present for your community. As an all-boys school, we also give special attention to talking about healthy forms of masculinity and how to be your best self in a society that often sends mixed signals to boys. In a world where soft skills are going underdeveloped, we make time to exercise and showcase presentation skills, community service, introspective thought, and vulnerability.

A Way To Embrace Your Passions and Push Them Further

As a matter of practice, Theodate's philosophy of education led her to an unusual approach to instruction. She rejected a rote, one-size-fits-all approach to education.

> *The use of library books instead of a single text will be encouraged in every department and should be effective at once in such fields as history, English, science, and mathematics, among the major subjects. Thus, each boy will not study parrot-like the same book that is being studied by*

> *any other boy, but he will seek out information in many different books, using what might be called the research method. This will make our boys excited about things of the mind, a feeling which is desirable above all else. Each boy will also be encouraged to carry forward one major piece of work during each year. This may be the writing of a book or essay, it may be a poetic translation or a prose adaptation, or it may fall into entirely different fields, becoming the scientific keeping of poultry, the building of a boat, or the making of a painting.*

This was more than just fanciful thinking on the part of our founder.

Consider, for example, this from Pete Seeger '36:

> *One of the advantages of progressive education is that if there is a problem, figuring out how to solve it is a fun job. Instead of looking it up in a book, start imagining this – start imagining that. It's true, you may be just reinventing the wheel. You could do it quicker, perhaps, if you got the book, but it's good to get practice.*

Each year, a student pursues a program of studies consisting of at least five classes, including at least four core subjects chosen from the following disciplines: art, English, engineering and computer science, history, mathematics, science, and world language. In the 2025–26 school year, Avon Old Farms offered a course catalog of 116 classes – 28 of which are in visual or performing arts.

Few schools blend tradition and innovation as intentionally as Avon. As national standards evolved through the mid-20th century, Avon held tightly to Theodate's ethos by finding new ways to offer student-driven intellectual exploration. In 2014, Chair of the Visual Arts Department Cristina Pinton set out to create a program for advanced artists who she thought would benefit from a sustained length of time in the afternoons dedicated to developing their portfolios. It was called the Afternoon Independent Project program.

Since then, the program has evolved to include students pursuing a variety of interests. Now known as the Advanced Independent Project (AIP) program, students work under the expertise of professionals both on and off campus to complete a significant project or series of projects and then present what he learned to the entire student body. Given the space to experience a trade with the guidance of trained and proven adults, students build their resume and gain invaluable experience as they seek further education in that field. Internships in medicine and finance and intensive studies in art and laboratory science have featured prominently in the AIP program over the years.

While at Avon, Cam was an active student who joined the robotics program as a developer, took computer science and technology courses, and used the AIP program to explore engineering and mobile app development with guidance from teachers and industry mentors. Illustrating how it works in the real world today, Cam recently shared,

> *Avon played a major role in my personal growth by giving me the freedom to dive deep into my interests, explore new passions, and by creating an environment where I stepped outside my comfort zone every day. It's a unique experience, as you engage with your teachers and peers in a much more*

personal and connected way with real chances to explore new ideas and possibilities. At Avon, I learned to take smart risks and seize opportunities, and those are habits I've carried into both my personal and professional life.

He matriculated to the University of Maryland where he earned a degree in computer science and upon graduation became a software engineer with Microsoft. Today, he's a machine learning engineer with Meta.

As many have done, Avon has also built in a week's worth of time dedicated to topics outside the realm of the traditional classroom. Theodate strongly believed that students should work alongside faculty mentors to produce meaningful work. Our Intersession program honors that tradition by offering courses that are often team-taught by faculty and staff on topics outside of the standard curriculum, but nonetheless relevant and centered on the R.E.A.L. Learning model. Intersession extends the classroom and opens the academic schedule to allow students and faculty to explore a topic of interest in greater detail with an experiential component since field trips and project-based learning feature prominently in the courses. Each spring, students choose from a list of 50+ courses to try their hand at something new. Whether they enroll in blacksmithing or marine biology, the students are fully-immersed in what are most often off-campus experiences for a week dedicated to the pursuit of trying something new.

Additionally, Avon has done something we believe few others have: we've hosted three academic conferences, complete with paper proposals, presentations, and keynote speakers. As the host location, our students not only attend the conference as audience members, they present original work as well. How often are high schoolers able to put on their resume "presented original work at an academic conference"?

> *Avon created an environment of opportunity and support, and that was evident from the faculty to the brotherhood. This environment enabled me to take chances and bet on myself; this learned behavior has become part of my personality. You do not know what you are capable of until you apply yourself and put your best foot forward.*
>
> – Alumnus, Aaron

Communal Living: The Culture of Caring for the Whole Boy

What's most curious about private school communities is that while it's easy to see the student body as one unit who likely are cut from the same cloth and are all heading in the same direction, the abundance of unique individuals you encounter in any given year is incredibly vast. And, as a school of 400 students and 150 faculty, somehow they each find a place in our brotherhood that is uniquely theirs, an intersection of outlets that cater to his individual needs and interests. The outdoorsmen commune in Nimrod Cabin, blaze trails through our 800+ acres, share cabin suppers under the pavilion each Tuesday night, and serve the greater community each week chopping wood, decorating for the holidays, and more.

Those seeking fellowship and understanding of the Lord come together for Bible Study on Thursday nights in Pelican 23 – no longer an English classroom, but a space of faith. The young man who just recently found his voice joins the Singed Beavers and practices a cappella singing with a group of similarly talented individuals after study hall in the choir practice room. And, somehow, one student finds the time and commitment for each one of these because they are important to him and give him purpose and strength.

In addition to finding space for individual interests and needs, one thing that bonds our students – across generations – are the shared responsibilities that make our community successful. The minutes of that first faculty meeting led by Theodate indicate that the school would operate as a village, with a store, a post office, and a bank at which each boy would keep his own account. The school also depended upon each student completing his job – whether that be waiting tables at dinner or sweeping up after a meal, tending to the chickens and cows or editing the school newspaper. While it may be hard to see, these jobs are another aspect of holistic education: in teaching responsibility and self-management, boys leave school better prepared to take on the real world with confidence. Today, school jobs persist – we still have dinner waiters, but Tech Crew counts too – and are a key element of building character and grit: if you don't show up for your job, one of your brothers will need to fill your place.

Avonians also show up en masse in loud moments and in quiet ones. Many will be familiar with the Avon Army when it fills the stands of a football or hockey game, often with painted faces, Hawaiian shirts, and bullhorns. Fewer know that the Avon Army often also shows up in coats and school ties, somber and respectful, when a brother loses a family member. It shows up at weddings and at hospital rooms. It shows up in your inbox when you're home sick, and it shows up in your inbox when you get a promotion at work. Whether it's in celebration or in support, the Avon Army shows up for its brothers.

At the End of the Day, We Win and Lose Together

It's no secret that Avon Old Farms has a reputation as being a strong sports school. And while we know we have a lot more to offer than strong athletics, we do take pride in the school spirit our teams are able to evoke. Aside from training the physical body, however, once again Theodate set the groundwork for physical education as a way to teach the whole boy.

Sports build leadership, teamwork, resilience, and forge bonds through shared adversity.

Recently, Head Football Coach Jon Wholley gave a victory speech after winning the New England championship game. It was a great speech, but above his words, two things made it even more impactful: first, he gave the speech to the entire student body, who he commanded effortlessly to take a knee alongside his players since the entire school followed his lead with respect. Second, in his speech, he was able to reflect on a Compass Talk he had given weeks earlier: we win and lose together. Not as a team or as a program, but as a school, we had won that game. Each member of the brotherhood was a part of that victory, and it was one that they would hold on to dearly forever. A few weeks later, a senior gave his Chapel Talk and said,

> *Before Avon, life was about me: my friends, my family, my dogs, my lacrosse tournaments. At Avon, life became about us: our community, our competitions, our school spirit, our shared experiences.*

It was clear in that moment that our message of community has hit home.

Nothing is better than when pride surges after a big win, and the entire brotherhood comes together in celebration, chanting the school song, proudly declaring to be Men of Avon. Written by faculty member Paul Cushing in 1941, our song embodies what it means to be a Man of Avon:

Strike the drumhead, fly the banner
Youth leaps forward, like a wave
Sweeping all that's bad before it,

Build the future for the brave.
Thwart the foolish, guard the prudent,
Strike out boldly for the right:
Keep this land the home of freedom
Where all men may take delight.
Make our school and make our nation
Into places where, secure,
Lawfulness will find a haven
And where peace will long endure.
Now we gather, Men of Avon,
Men of honor, men of will,
Set our hearts upon the mountains,
And our destiny fulfill.

Closing

Avon's structure – its daily schedule, advisory, residential life, and academic programs – reflect an intentionally designed ecosystem for whole-boy development. It is a place where tradition fuels innovation, where character is cultivated as deliberately as intellect, and where boys learn to aspire boldly and persevere together. The village Theodate envisioned a century ago has become a living model of what holistic, student-centered education can achieve: a community that challenges, supports, and inspires young men to become thoughtful leaders and compassionate brothers. In celebrating its first hundred years, Avon Old Farms stands as a testament to what is possible when a school remains unwaveringly committed to knowing boys deeply and helping them grow into the very best versions of themselves.

The Oxford Academy

Location: Westbrook, Connecticut

Year Founded: 1906

Grades Served: 9–12 + Post Grad

Total Enrollment: Boys, 42

Percent Boarding: 100%

Percent Non-White: 20%

Percent From Out of State: 80%

Percent From Out of Country: 30%

2025–26 School Year Tuition: $88,000

Percent Who Receive Financial Aid: 10%

School Website: www.oxfordacademy.net

Head of School: Phil Cocchiola

The Oxford Academy

Chapter Completed By
Phil Cocchiola, Head of School

An Oxford Academy Education: Like Flying a Fighter Jet

What if I told you that an Oxford Academy education is akin to flying a fighter jet? What would you think? Well, believe it or not, the comparison is not as far-fetched as you might imagine.

Imagine the process of flying a fighter jet: precision, adaptability, rapid decision-making under pressure, and an unwavering understanding of both the machine and the mission. A fighter pilot must undergo rigorous training not only to master complex systems but to refine instincts, hone focus, and cultivate discipline. There's no "average" fighter pilot; each is a specialist, trained with intensity and intentionality.

Now, imagine if we trained every pilot the same way, using the same gear, same cockpit dimensions, same assumptions about who they are and how they learn. The result? Failure. And yet, for generations, that is how many schools have treated education, designing curricula, classrooms, and assessments around an imagined "average" student.

But not here.

At The Oxford Academy, we reject the notion of average. Our founding in 1906 by Dr. Joseph Weidberg was grounded in a revolutionary idea: that the best education starts not with a curriculum, but with a student. Rather than expecting students to conform to a one-size-fits-all system, Oxford built a system that conforms to the student. A system that meets the learner where he is and equips him to rise.

Each boy at Oxford is trained in his own aircraft, so to speak. We don't just design the cockpit to fit him; we teach him how to fly. This is education as it should be: responsive, intentional, demanding, and transformative. Every knob, every lever, every component of the cockpit is designed with the pilot in mind. In the same way, our teachers and mentors tailor each academic experience to the individual student's strengths, interests, and aspirations. This is not about making education easier; it's about making it meaningful.

And this is no metaphorical indulgence. Like a pilot-in-training, each Oxford student is asked to perform at high altitude, academically, socially, and emotionally. We challenge our boys to take ownership of their education. We train them in the Socratic Method, where inquiry matters more than answers and where dialogue refines thought. We ask them to engage, to take risks, to wrestle with complexity, and to emerge not with memorized facts, but with hard-won wisdom. This method, rooted in ancient philosophy, remains astonishingly modern. In a world of rapid information and shallow conclusions, the ability to ask good questions and think deeply is nothing short of revolutionary.

The Oxford student learns that learning is not a passive process; it's active, dynamic, and even thrilling. Like a flight mission, it requires preparation, execution, and reflection. There will be turbulence. There will be days when the headwinds seem too strong. But through it all, our boys come to understand the deeper truth: that difficulty is not a detour from learning, it is the path. Just as a pilot cannot avoid the occasional storm, a student must confront challenges to grow. We do not shelter our students from struggle. We help them navigate through it.

And where does this flight take place? On a campus like no other. Nestled beside the waters of the Long Island Sound and the Connecticut River, with sailboats dotting the horizon and seabirds overhead, our school feels like a runway to the world. Here, tides meet time-honored tradition. Mornings begin with light over the water, evenings close with quiet reflection by the docks. The setting reminds us that learning, like water, is fluid, deep, and always moving. And sometimes, when the clouds part just right, you can look out over the sound and feel the vastness of possibility.

Indeed, our location is more than picturesque; it's essential. Our proximity to water fosters a natural rhythm in our days and underscores the connection between inner balance and external environment. Our beaches are not just a physical space; they're a reflective one. They offer perspective, calm, and a reminder that the most powerful journeys often begin in stillness.

Our school motto, "Know Thyself," anchors this entire approach. Each young man here embarks on a journey of deep self-discovery. Through individualized instruction, consistent mentorship, and a carefully cultivated environment, we help each student uncover his strengths, confront his weaknesses, and clarify his sense of purpose. This is not education as a transaction; it is education as a transformation. A flight not only across subjects but inward, toward meaning, identity, and truth.

At Oxford, we don't view education as a conveyor belt toward some generic definition of success. We view it as a runway, each boy preparing for liftoff, each on a different trajectory, each discovering the unique contours of his potential. Some may ascend quickly, others more gradually. Some may change course midair. But each is given the tools to fly his own flight plan.

And this is possible because we insist on building everything, from lesson plans to relationships around the individual. Our 1:1 model is not a gimmick. It is the heart of our mission. It allows us to see each boy clearly. Not as a number, not as a data point, not as a standardized test score, but as a whole person. A student. A thinker. A dreamer. A pilot in training. This focus on the individual redefines the role of the teacher from one who delivers knowledge to one who draws out potential.

At the heart of an Oxford Academy education lie our core values: Respect, Integrity, Kindness, Community, and Civility. These aren't just words on a banner or themes for a campaign; they are living principles, intentionally woven into every aspect of life at Oxford. They guide how we treat one another, how we resolve conflict, how we support each other through challenges, and how we grow.

These values are cultivated through our Character and Leadership Curriculum (CLC) a unique, seminar-based program that anchors our emphasis on social-emotional development and personal well-being. Meeting weekly in small groups, the CLC is a space where honest, respectful communication is encouraged and modeled. Students are empowered to speak openly, listen thoughtfully, and reflect meaningfully on their experiences.

The CLC is not a scripted program. It evolves with the student. Younger boys begin with foundational skills: managing routines, engaging in self-care, exploring their role in the weekend community. As they grow, so too does the curriculum, emphasizing independent living, leadership within the dorms, and accountability to others. It's a program designed not only to help students navigate Oxford, but to prepare them to thrive far beyond it.

In a school where half of the faculty live on campus, these values come to life in real time. Students see them in action during meals, dorm check-ins, weekend trips, and casual hallway conversations. Teachers are not distant figures; they are mentors, role models, and neighbors. This immersive community allows us to focus on improving habits in a genuine and sustained way. And when every adult is working from the same foundation of shared values, the impact is transformative.

At Oxford, we don't just talk about character, we build it, one conversation, one interaction, and one small act of leadership at a time.

But there's another vital aspect to our model: the power of a single-gender environment. In a world full of distractions and expectations, boys often face unique challenges in developing confidence, communication, and a strong sense of self. At Oxford, our all-boys setting creates a space where students can drop the pretense and embrace the process of becoming. Without the pressure to perform or conform, they learn to be authentic. They learn to lead. They learn to listen. Here, vulnerability is strength, and growth is expected. In this environment, boys are free to explore every aspect of who they are becoming.

Think for a moment about the cockpit again. Imagine how dangerous it would be to send a young man into the sky with controls he doesn't understand, or instruments that don't reflect his physiology. In the same way, how can we expect boys to succeed when they are handed textbooks they don't connect with, teaching styles that don't fit their minds, and expectations that ignore their individuality? The results are predictable: disengagement, frustration, and a loss of confidence.

Oxford refuses to make that compromise.

We are committed to crafting each educational experience with precision and care. We adjust the dials. We calibrate the instruments. We check in constantly. And, most importantly, we trust our students to learn to fly, not just with our help, but eventually on their own. Independence is not given; it is earned through preparation, trust, and resilience. We believe in our boys long before they believe in themselves.

No one becomes a pilot overnight. Nor does anyone become educated in a single term or even a single year. It is a process. A sacred process. And it is one that demands patience, skill, humility, and belief. True education takes time. It requires mentoring, failure, perseverance, and reflection. We honor that journey.

Our faculty are not just instructors; they are flight instructors. They don't hand out pre-made maps. They help our boys draw their own. They model integrity, perseverance, and curiosity. They teach our students how to navigate not just the classroom, but life. They teach our boys that knowledge is not static; it must be earned, tested, and applied. And when a student stumbles, as all do, our faculty does not judge; they guide.

What truly sets Oxford apart is not just the caliber of our educators but their commitment to living the mission. Over half of our faculty live on campus, many with their spouses, children, even pets – and this simple fact changes everything. At most boarding schools, students and teachers cross paths in classrooms or during scheduled office hours. At Oxford, they live side by side. Faculty serve not only as teachers but as dorm parents, mentors, coaches, and trusted adults present in the quiet and unplanned moments of the day. They are there for the early morning breakfast (which also happens to be individualized) in the dining hall, the late-night questions, the impromptu games of catch or chess. The boys see their teachers as whole people, modeling balance, kindness, and accountability, and in return, the faculty come to know each boy not just as a learner, but as a person.

This model fosters a depth of relationship that is rare and profoundly impactful. It creates a sense of safety and belonging, not by policy, but by presence. When a boy is struggling, there is someone nearby who already knows him, his story, his humor, his fears, his strengths. And because many of our faculty stay for years, often decades, they become institutional memory-bearers, keepers of tradition, and builders of continuity in a world that too often feels transient and fractured. Their longevity offers the boys something immeasurable: trust built over time, consistency, and the comforting knowledge that the adults around them are invested for the long haul. This deeply rooted faculty presence is part of why Oxford feels less like an institution and more like a home.

And it's in this community where the power of integrated character and social development shines. Through advisory groups, counseling support, service learning, and student leadership, Oxford helps each young man not only understand his intellect but also develop his heart. Respect, empathy, and emotional intelligence are not extras here; they are embedded in the fabric of everyday life. We believe that character is not separate from scholarship; it is its foundation.

Our history also fuels our future. With over a century of experience, Oxford has weathered wars, revolutions in education, societal shifts, and technological transformations. And through it all, our mission has remained constant: to educate each boy as an individual and to prepare him for a meaningful life. This long-standing tradition is not about being old-fashioned; it's about being rooted. Our deep roots give us the confidence to innovate, and our legacy gives students the assurance that they are part of something enduring.

And Let's Not Forget the Stories.

Take John, who arrived here unsure of his academic ability, quiet in seminar, hesitant to raise his hand. Over months, through patient mentorship, encouragement, and the one-on-one relationships that define this place, he found his voice. He began asking questions that reshaped entire classroom conversations. Or consider Charlie, who once struggled to write a paragraph. Today, he is drafting college essays that reflect a mind matured by challenge and lifted by guidance. These boys didn't just pass through Oxford; they were changed by it.

One might think that our unique one-on-one model might confine a young man's growth as they move forward towards college and larger group settings, but this couldn't be further from the truth. When someone knows how they learn and is given ample opportunities to collaborate through group activities such as labs, public speaking opportunities, and specifically designed classroom experiences, they leave with an advantage over their peers. In fact, it is not uncommon for our graduates to share that they have established relationships with their college professors, as for them, it has become second nature to self-advocate with a teacher.

And Let's Not Forget the Value of Community.

Fighter pilots, for all their solo training, rely on a squadron. They rely on ground crews, on air traffic control, and on trusted teammates who understand the mission. In the same way, Oxford boys never fly alone. They are part of a brotherhood, a close-knit community where collaboration, respect, and shared values keep them grounded even as they ascend. Dorm life, house meetings, mealtime conversations; these are more than traditions; they are essential moments of connection, where boys become young men, and classmates become brothers.

One of the most defining features of The Oxford Academy is our inclusive yet fiercely competitive athletic program. Every student participates. Period. We don't hold tryouts. We don't cut players. Instead, we embrace a philosophy rooted in opportunity, believing that every young man, regardless of prior experience or perceived ability, deserves the chance to contribute to a team. And when given that chance, remarkable things happen.

Time and again, we've seen students who never considered themselves "athletes" step onto the field or court and discover new strength, grit, and resilience. We've watched young men learn how to lead, how to fail gracefully, how to support their teammates, and how to rise after setbacks. We've seen shy students become captains, and quiet boys make the game-winning play. Our teams are more than collections of players; they are families. And because we include everyone, our definition of success expands. Yes, we compete. Yes, we win. But our greatest victories happen when a student who doubted himself finds courage in the game.

This commitment to inclusive excellence is unusual in boarding schools, and it underscores our belief that growth comes through participation. Every boy wears the jersey. Every boy learns what it means to prepare, to strive, to persevere. Athletics, at Oxford, are not extracurricular; they are essential training grounds for character.

We also believe in the power of play. Of movement. Of fresh air. Our afternoons and weekends are filled with competition and camaraderie: kayaking, paddleboarding, pickup basketball, trail hikes, ultimate frisbee matches, and impromptu games of chess on the lawn. These activities, often spontaneous and always spirited, are where boys learn balance. They remind us that healthy minds thrive in healthy bodies, and that joy is not separate from learning; it is essential to it.

There is also the quiet, powerful influence of our traditions and rituals that have been passed down over decades and still shape the identity of our community. Morning meetings, 100 nights to graduation celebration, international and domestic travel, Cape Cod whale watching, maple sugaring, beekeeping, and many, many others. These moments mark time and transformation. They provide rhythm for our year and remind each student that he is part of something larger, something lasting.

And when they need a moment of stillness, they walk to the water, sit on the beach, or watch the sailboats tack into the wind, small reminders that learning and life both follow the rhythms of nature. The brackish scent of the tide, the creak of mooring lines, the occasional bell buoy sounding in the distance, these are not distractions. They are part of the cadence of this place, the quiet background music to every breakthrough.

It's this unity, this sense of belonging, that gives our boys the courage to risk. To fail. To get back up. To try again. Because real education doesn't eliminate failure, it reframes it as a vital part of growth. At Oxford, we normalize struggle. We affirm that getting lost in thought is not a sign of weakness; it's the first step toward insight. We celebrate not just achievement, but effort. Not just answers, but inquiry. Not just progress, but persistence.

Every essay, every seminar, every late-night dorm conversation contributes to the development of a young man who not only knows how to learn but knows why learning matters. A young man who understands that education isn't about performing for others – it's about discovering who he is, what he stands for, and where he is meant to go. When our students leave, they carry with them more than a diploma. They carry a vision, a purpose, and the tools to pursue both.

At other schools, students often feel like passengers. At Oxford, they are at the controls. They set the course, adjust the trajectory, and respond to the winds of challenge and change. And by the time they graduate, they don't just leave with transcripts, they leave with a compass. That compass points not to conformity, but to calling. Not to comfort, but to courage.

What we are doing here is not just education, it is formation. Formation of character. Of intellect. Of will. Of soul. We are in the business of transformation. And the evidence is all around us: alumni who lead with humility, serve with integrity, and live with purpose. These men return not just with gratitude, but with impact. Some become educators themselves, inspired to carry the torch. Others enter service, law, medicine, or the arts, propelled by a sense of direction first kindled on this campus.

Many of our alumni go on to become extraordinarily successful, not only by society's traditional metrics, but in terms of personal fulfillment, leadership, and service. From CEOs to diplomats, authors to entrepreneurs, physicians to filmmakers, our graduates are making their mark across the globe. Even more importantly, they remember where they came from. They return to campus, support the community, speak at commencement, or simply offer advice, and help our boys envision paths they never knew existed. To be an Oxford student is to have access to an inspiring, generous, and deeply accomplished network of men who know firsthand the value of this place. They are living proof that an Oxford education prepares you not only to take off, but to soar.

This is what makes Oxford different. Not just the methods, but the mission.

We do not produce products. We are launching future leaders.

We are not delivering content. We are developing character.

We are not chasing averages. We are cultivating excellence in all its personal, powerful, unpredictable forms. Excellence is not defined by test scores or trophies, but by the steady, quiet strength of a man who knows himself, serves others, and leads by example.

So, next time you think about what it means to "go to school," don't picture rows of desks and bells between classes. Picture something bolder. Picture a boy climbing into his own cockpit, hands steady on the controls, eyes on the horizon. Picture him learning not just facts, but how to think, how to speak, how to lead. Picture him questioning, wrestling, soaring. Picture the moment when he realizes the skies aren't a limit, they're a beginning.

And when you picture him, see the sun glinting off the water behind him. Feel the pull of tide and time as they carry him forward. Watch as he walks toward class with the quiet confidence of someone who knows who he is, where he's going, and what he stands for.

That, too, is Oxford.

That's what we do here. That's what we've always done.

The Oxford Academy – leading the charge against average.

See you in the skies and on the water.

Chapter 19

Conclusion

Part I: What Became Visible

All of the schools included in this book elevate the student experience beyond a baseline that is too often accepted as sufficient. They are here because, in different ways and in different contexts, each has made intentional choices about how young people live, learn, belong, and grow. What follows is not an assessment of relative strength among them, nor an attempt to distinguish "better" from "best." It is an exploration of how elevation takes shape and what becomes visible when a school community commits, collectively and seriously, to educating the whole person.

When we began this project we resisted the urge to decide in advance what we were looking for. That restraint was deliberate. We wanted schools to speak first – to describe themselves in their own language and on their own terms – without being sorted prematurely into categories or evaluated against a fixed rubric. Only after living with these chapters – reading them closely, noticing their repetitions as well as their differences – did certain patterns begin to surface.

These patterns were not imposed. They emerged through accumulation.

Coherence as a Shared Commitment

Across very different schools, one of the most consistent qualities was coherence. Not uniformity of approach, but visible and lived alignment between values and daily practice. In these communities, what adults said they cared about showed up, again and again, in schedules, expectations, relationships, and routines.

This coherence did not depend on novelty. Few of these schools were defined by a single innovative program or signature initiative. Instead, they tended to make a smaller number of commitments and then sustain them over time. The work was often quiet and repetitive: maintaining expectations, revisiting norms, reinforcing culture, and resisting pressures to drift.

Coherence, in this sense, is not a static achievement but an ongoing practice. It requires attention, discipline, and the willingness to make tradeoffs. Across contexts, it became clear that elevation does not come from adding more, but from aligning what already exists.

Responsibility as Part of Daily Life

Another shared feature across these schools was the way responsibility was woven into the fabric of daily life. Responsibility was not framed as a future outcome – something students would acquire later, once they were "ready." It was treated as a developmental practice, cultivated through real roles, real expectations, and real consequences.

This took many forms. Some schools emphasized work programs or shared labor. Others highlighted student governance, peer accountability, or community norms that carried weight. The particulars differed, but the underlying message was consistent: students are not merely recipients of education; they are participants in sustaining the communities they inhabit.

Importantly, responsibility was not equated with independence. Support was visible and ongoing. Boundaries were clear. Adults remained involved. What distinguished these environments was not the absence of structure, but the way responsibility and support were held together rather than traded off.

Structure as a Condition for Growth

In popular discourse, holistic or progressive education is often associated with looseness or informality. The chapters in this book complicate that narrative. While structures varied widely, all of these schools treated structure as a necessary condition for growth.

Schedules, routines, and expectations were not primarily about control. They were about creating predictability, clarity, and safety – conditions under which students could take meaningful risks and practice autonomy without being overwhelmed. Structure, in this sense, functioned as care.

Where structure was strong, schools described the adult labor required to sustain it: consistency, follow-through, and presence. Where it was evolving, schools named the tension openly. Across contexts, elevation did not come from removing structure, but from its intentional design.

Adult Presence as Cultural Work

One of the most consistent elements across these chapters was the role of adults – not as distant authorities or specialized service providers, but as visible, engaged members of the community. Adults were present across settings: in classrooms, residences, shared spaces, and informal moments where culture is reinforced or eroded.

This kind of presence is demanding. It requires adults to hold authority without relying on coercion, to model accountability without perfection, and to stay engaged even when outcomes are uncertain. It also requires institutions to support adults in doing this work collectively, rather than depending on individual charisma or heroics.

Across schools, adult presence emerged as a form of moral architecture. It shaped what was possible – not through control, but through consistency and relationship.

Community as a Site of Learning

In every school included here, education extended beyond formal instruction. Learning continued in dormitories, studios, kitchens, fields, and shared spaces, where students practiced negotiation, empathy, leadership, and repair in real time.

Community was not romanticized. Conflict, disagreement, and failure were common. What mattered was how those moments were handled. Rather than being treated as disruptions to education, they were understood as part of it.

When community is treated as a site of learning, education becomes participatory rather than transactional. Knowledge and skills still matter deeply, but they are situated within relationships that give them consequence and meaning.

Difference Without Hierarchy

Perhaps the most striking realization, taken as a whole, was that difference did not undermine cohesion. The schools in this book vary widely in philosophy, population, scale, and setting. Some are small and intimate; others are large and complex. Some are explicitly progressive; others operate within more traditional frames.

These chapters were written by schools, not by students. That choice reflects the purpose of the project: to understand how institutions conceive of their work, articulate their values, and describe the environments they are actively trying to sustain. Within that shared frame, schools made different choices about voice and representation. Some chapters include student quotations or reflections; others speak entirely through institutional language. This variation is inherent to the unstructured invitation to participate, but should not be interpreted as evaluative.

Institutional narratives, whether interwoven with student voice or not, reflect intention, structure, and self-understanding. They do not – and cannot – capture the full range of individual experience within those environments. Adolescence is uneven by nature, and even within coherent communities, experiences of belonging, challenge, or fit will differ. The presence of thoughtful design does not guarantee a uniform experience, nor does the absence of quoted student voice imply it was not available.

This book does not claim to offer a comprehensive account of student life, nor does it attempt to adjudicate between institutional intent and individual outcome. What it offers instead is a view of how schools understand the moral and developmental responsibilities they hold, and how those understandings are translated into daily structure and expectation. Elevation, as described here, is not a promise of perfection, but a commitment to coherence – one that remains subject to interpretation, lived experience, and ongoing accountability.

And yet, that variation did not fragment the collection. It clarified it.

What unified these schools was not a shared model, but a shared seriousness about adolescence and education. Each had found its own way to elevate the student experience beyond a minimal or transactional conception of schooling. The differences among them reflect context, choice, and history – not relative worth.

That realization only became visible through sequence and attention. It could not have been named in advance.

Part II: What It Takes to Elevate a School

If Part I describes what became visible when these schools were allowed to speak for themselves, Part II turns toward a harder question: what does it actually take to build, and sustain, this kind of educational environment?

The answer, across contexts, was neither glamorous nor easily transferable. Elevation, as it appeared in these schools, was not the result of a single program, philosophy, or charismatic leader. It emerged instead from a sustained commitment to coherence, carried forward through countless small decisions made over time. What distinguished these communities was less what they added than what they protected.

Coherence Is Labor

Coherence does not maintain itself. Across schools, it became clear that alignment between values and practice requires ongoing work – often invisible, frequently repetitive, and rarely celebrated. Coherence depends not only on intentional design around a shared set of values, but also on sustained labor. Presence, consistency, and relational authority are not abstract qualities; they are enacted daily by adults whose work is emotionally demanding, time-intensive, and largely unseen. Schools that rely solely on individual commitment or charismatic leadership without also attending to adult sustainability risk eroding the very coherence they seek to preserve. What distinguished many of the communities in this book was not the absence of strain, but the degree to which responsibility for culture was held collectively, supported structurally, and renewed over time.

This work shows up in how adults respond to predictable pressures: a parent request that conflicts with stated norms, a market trend that promises growth at the expense of fit, a student situation that invites an easier exception rather than a harder conversation. Elevation, in these moments, depended on whether institutions were willing to act in accordance with their stated commitments even when doing so was inconvenient.

In practice, this meant revisiting expectations repeatedly, repairing drift when it occurred, and accepting that clarity sometimes comes at the cost of short-term comfort. The schools in this book did not eliminate contradiction. They learned to live with it deliberately.

Saying No Is Part of the Work

One of the least visible but most consequential aspects of coherence was the willingness to say no. Not just to individual requests, but to opportunities that promised expansion, recognition, or ease without alignment.

Saying no took many forms: declining to grow beyond a sustainable size, resisting pressure to broaden mission for market appeal, or holding boundaries around student readiness and support. These decisions were rarely framed as moral victories. They were described as difficult, ongoing negotiations between aspiration and capacity.

What became clear is that elevation often requires constraint. Schools that attempted to be everything to everyone struggled to maintain clarity. Those that protected a more limited scope were better able to deliver on what they promised.

Adult Consistency Over Time

Across schools, adult consistency emerged as one of the most significant, and fragile, contributors to elevation. Consistency did not mean rigidity or uniformity. It meant that students could rely on adults to respond in ways that were predictable, principled, and grounded in shared expectations.

This kind of consistency is hard to sustain. It requires alignment among adults, institutional memory, and structures that support collective decision-making rather than isolated discretion. It also requires schools to attend to adult well-being, turnover, and support, recognizing that culture is not transmitted automatically.

Where adult consistency held, students described feeling known, trusted, and accountable. Where it faltered, schools named the work required to repair it. Elevation, in this sense, depended as much on adult culture as on student programming.

Responsibility Cannot Be Delegated Away

Another pattern that emerged was the refusal to outsource responsibility for adolescent development. While these schools made use of specialized support where appropriate, they did not treat responsibility, belonging, or growth as problems to be managed by external systems alone.

Instead, responsibility was distributed across the community. Faculty, residential staff, administrators, and students themselves shared in the work of maintaining norms, addressing conflict, and supporting growth. This distribution was not always efficient. It was, however, formative.

Elevation, it became clear, is compromised when responsibility is fragmented – when students experience their lives as a series of disconnected interventions rather than a coherent environment.

Time as a Necessary Ingredient

Finally, elevation required time. Not just in the sense of longer days or residential immersion, but in the willingness to let growth unfold without rushing outcomes. These schools were attentive to pacing – academic, social, and emotional – and wary of equating speed with success.

This orientation runs counter to many contemporary pressures. Families and institutions alike often seek visible progress, measurable gains, and rapid resolution. The schools in this book resisted that impulse where they could, trusting that development is uneven and that meaningful growth rarely follows a linear timeline.

Time, in this sense, was not a luxury. It was a design choice.

The Cost of Coherence

Taken together, these observations point toward a sobering conclusion: elevation is demanding. It requires clarity, restraint, adult discipline, and a tolerance for ambiguity. It asks institutions to accept limits, absorb tension, and commit to work that does not always produce immediate or marketable results.

None of the schools in this book claimed to have mastered this work. All described it as ongoing. What they shared was a willingness to engage it seriously, rather than treating holistic education as an aspiration divorced from institutional reality.

There is not a singular formula for elevation, but there is certainly a cost, or perhaps an investment, which only matures and compounds over time, through sustained attention, restraint, and care.

Part III: Limits, Power, and the Responsibility to Choose

Any serious discussion of education must eventually confront questions of power. Who has access to particular kinds of learning environments? Who gets to decide what counts as a "good" education? And what responsibilities accompany institutions that have the ability – financial, cultural, or structural – to shape young people's lives in sustained and consequential ways? The schools in this book do not escape these questions. Nor should they.

Situated Excellence

Boarding schools exist within specific historical, economic, and cultural contexts. They are shaped by tuition models, philanthropic structures, regulatory environments, and long-standing traditions. These conditions create both possibility and constraint. While many of the schools in this book work intentionally to broaden access through financial aid, outreach, and mission-driven enrollment, none operate outside the realities of inequality.

Recognizing this does not negate the work being done. It situates it.

Schools like those described here are shaped not only by design and intention, but also by selection. The admissions process, however mission-driven, is inherently exclusionary, and the coherence visible within these communities depends in part on student fit and readiness, and a family's capacity to support a school's expectations over time. This reality does not negate the seriousness of the work described in these chapters, nor does it render claims of inclusion disingenuous. It does, however, set realistic limits on what can be generalized. What travels most reliably from these schools is not a replicable form, but an understanding of how intentional communities align values, structure, and responsibility once participation has been chosen.

The mistake is not in acknowledging excellence within a bounded context, but in mistaking that context for universality. The schools included here elevate the student experience in meaningful ways, and they do so within particular conditions that cannot be easily replicated at scale. Treating them as prototypes for wholesale reform risks flattening both their achievements and their limitations.

The Difference Between Influence and Replication

It is tempting, especially in moments of educational dissatisfaction, to look for models that can be adopted, exported, or scaled. This book resists that impulse deliberately. The schools described here are not blueprints. They are case studies in intentionality.

What may travel are not programs or structures, but questions: How are values translated into daily practice? Where is responsibility placed? How is authority exercised? What tradeoffs are accepted and which are refused? Influence, in this sense, is not about copying form. It is about interrogating function. See **Appendix B** for additional framing questions.

Power, Held or Avoided

Institutions that work closely with adolescents hold a particular kind of power. They shape not only academic trajectories, but identities, habits, and understandings of belonging. The schools in this book varied in how explicitly they named this power, but all were shaped by it.

Residential educational environments intensify proximity, authority, and influence. That intimacy can deepen care and belonging, but it also magnifies risk. Seriousness about power therefore includes not only intention and relationship, but guardrails: clear boundaries, accountability structures, and mechanisms for reporting, repair, and oversight. Coherence without such safeguards risks becoming coercive rather than supportive. Elevation, pursued responsibly, requires attending to both possibility and vulnerability with equal clarity.

What emerged was a shared understanding, sometimes implicit, that power cannot be abdicated. Choosing not to reflect on institutional influence does not remove it; it merely renders it less accountable. Elevation, when pursued seriously, requires institutions to examine not only what they provide, but what they privilege.

Adolescence and Moral Formation

Adolescence is not merely a preparatory phase on the way to adulthood; it is a period of life with its own moral and developmental claims. During these years young people are forming durable understandings of authority, responsibility, belonging, and self-worth – learning and development which often comes more from their daily experience in the world rather than explicit moments of instruction. Adolescence today unfolds within a landscape marked by rapid change, ambient uncertainty, and competing demands for attention, ricocheting between digital hyperconnection and social isolation. Asked to orient themselves amid forces that can feel vast or unresolved, their daily lives too often remain fragmented and disconnected from meaningful responsibility or belonging.

In this context, institutional choices carry disproportionate weight. How authority is exercised, how responsibility is shared, and how coherence is maintained are not abstract design questions; they are lived realities that actively shape how young people come to understand themselves, their relation to others, and their space and place in the world. Coherent educational communities – where expectations are clear, relationships are sustained, and participation carries real consequence – offer something increasingly rare: a lived experience of meaning, connection, and agency grounded in daily practice. To take adolescence seriously is to recognize that educational environments do not simply prepare students for the future; they participate actively in who students are becoming, right now.

Education is never neutral. Decisions about structure, freedom, discipline, and community participation shape how young people understand authority, agency, and responsibility. The schools in this book did not always agree on how best to navigate these questions, but they shared an understanding that adolescence is a formative period, not simply a transitional one.

This recognition carries weight. To design an educational environment is to make claims, both explicit and implicit, about what matters, who belongs, and how individuals relate to a collective. These claims deserve scrutiny, especially when made within institutions that enjoy relative autonomy. Taking responsibility here does not require certainty. It requires willingness.

Choosing Constraint

One of the most countercultural insights surfaced by this collection is that ethical education often involves choosing constraint rather than expansion. This applies not only to programmatic decisions, but to institutional posture more broadly.

Constraint can mean limiting growth, narrowing focus, or declining opportunities that dilute mission. It can also mean acknowledging where a school's approach is not appropriate for every student, every family, or every moment in a young person's life.

In a landscape that often rewards ambition without reflection, constraint becomes a moral choice.

Holding Tension Without Resolution

This book does not resolve the tensions it surfaces. It does not reconcile excellence with equity, autonomy with authority, or aspiration with access. What it offers instead is a way of holding those tensions without denying them.

The schools included here are not solutions. They are sites of ongoing negotiation between ideals and realities, between individual growth and collective responsibility, between what is possible and what is fair. Recognizing this does not weaken the project. It strengthens it.

What Responsibility Looks Like, Now

If this book has argued for anything, it is not a particular model of schooling, but a posture toward responsibility. Not responsibility as compliance, or as a burden to be shifted elsewhere, but responsibility as a willingness to choose with intention and to recognize that educational environments are designed, whether consciously or by default, and that those designs shape young lives in lasting ways.

These educational environments also exist within the context of family choice. For parents and caregivers, the decision to entrust a young person to a residential community is rarely simple or abstract. It involves hope, uncertainty, and real tradeoffs, along with a willingness to share the intimate and deeply personal responsibility of supporting an adolescent's growth with an institution whose influence extends far beyond academics and into the texture of daily life.

Naming this reality means acknowledging that families who choose a boarding education enter into a set of complicated – and sometimes competing – roles: partner and client, advocate and challenger, supporter and steward. These roles shift over time, shaped by strain, disagreement, understanding, trust, and alignment. Education, and especially education within a residential school, unfolds inside a network of relationships between student, school, and family – each bringing its own values, limits, and commitments to the shared work of supporting adolescent development. Simply acknowledging tension does not resolve it, but any honest understanding of boarding schools must recognize that it exists – and that a school's ability to enter into and work through that tension with the same coherence it brings to student life is critical to the health of the relationship.

In choosing a school, families are also choosing more than a setting or a set of outcomes. They are entering into relationship with an institutional stance toward adolescence itself – how young people are understood, how authority is exercised, how responsibility is practiced, and how community is sustained. That choice is rarely made with full certainty or perfect alignment, nor does it imply uniform agreement over time. It is, instead, an engagement with a moral framework that will shape daily experience in ways both visible and subtle. Naming this does not elevate one school over another; it clarifies what is at stake. Educational communities are not neutral containers oriented solely toward production or outcome. They are lived expressions of how adults understand adolescence, and choosing to participate in them is also a choice to live, for a time, within the values they enact.

For the schools in this book, responsibility begins with clarity. It shows up in the courage to articulate what a school is for, and just as importantly, what it is not. It requires resisting the gravitational pull of expansion for its own sake, the temptation to promise more than can be delivered with integrity, and the pressure to respond reactively to every new demand. Responsibility, here, is not about ambition; it is about alignment.

This kind of responsibility is demanding precisely because it is ongoing. It does not resolve itself through a single decision or declaration. It requires sustained attention: revisiting assumptions, repairing drift, and noticing when practice begins to outrun purpose. It asks adults, both individually and collectively, to remain accountable not only for outcomes, but for process: for how authority is exercised, how expectations are enforced, and how care is expressed when things go wrong.

Responsibility also involves acknowledging limits without retreating into defensiveness. The schools in this book operate within systems that confer advantage unevenly. To name this is not to invalidate the work being done, but to situate it ethically. Elevation that refuses to examine its own conditions risks becoming insulated from consequence.

At the same time, responsibility does not require paralysis. It does not demand that schools solve inequity writ large before acting with intention where they are. It asks instead for humility about impact, honesty about reach, and a willingness to remain in conversation with critique rather than dismiss it or absorb it unexamined.

For educators, responsibility may look like reclaiming coherence in environments fragmented by competing priorities. It may involve asking where values are being articulated without being lived, or where structure has been mistaken for rigidity or abandoned entirely. It may mean slowing down long enough to notice which practices are sustaining growth and which are merely performing it.

For institutional leaders, responsibility often takes the form of constraint. It is expressed in decisions to protect culture rather than scale, to invest in adult sustainability rather than short-term optics, and to tolerate complexity instead of oversimplifying it for external consumption. These choices are rarely rewarded immediately. Their effects are cumulative, subtle, and often invisible until they are absent.

For families and students, responsibility may involve resisting transactional narratives of education altogether. It may mean asking not only what outcomes a school promises, but what kind of daily experience it offers, how young people are expected to participate, contribute, and belong. It may involve choosing environments that demand engagement rather than consumption.

And for readers who arrive at this book without direct ties to boarding schools, responsibility may take a quieter form. It may show up as a shift in attention: noticing how educational spaces are designed, how adolescence is treated, and how authority operates in places where young people spend their time. It may involve asking better questions, rather than seeking faster answers.

What this book ultimately suggests is that responsibility in education is less about certainty than about care. It is not a fixed position one arrives at, but a stance one must keep choosing. Elevation, in this sense, is not an achievement to be claimed, but a practice to be maintained – one that matures slowly, through consistency, restraint, and a willingness to remain accountable to the people most affected by our decisions.

If these schools offer anything of value beyond their individual contexts, it is not a set of solutions, but a reminder: that when adults take responsibility seriously – when they design environments with intention, hold authority with care, and accept the costs of coherence – young people notice. And in noticing, they begin to learn not just how to succeed, but how to belong, contribute, and choose with integrity themselves.

Closing

This book did not begin as a theory, a study, or a search for definitive answers. It began with recognition. Two friends, working in and around schools, found themselves repeatedly drawn to a small number of educational communities where something felt different, more intentional, more coherent, more alive. We could not fully explain what we were seeing, but we recognized it when we encountered it. And we believed it was worth paying attention to.

The original aim of this project was, in some ways, modest: to capture these schools' stories in their own voices; to curate them thoughtfully rather than exhaustively; to place them in enough context to be legible; and to amplify them, not as exemplars to be copied, but as lived expressions of educational communities taking adolescence seriously.

What has emerged through that process is a clearer form of understanding, not imposed from the outside, but shaped by sustained attention. Taken together, these schools do not resolve into a single philosophy or model. They differ widely in structure, scale, population, and emphasis. What they share is not sameness, but seriousness: a commitment to elevating the student experience beyond a minimal or transactional conception of education.

That elevation does not come from novelty or prescription. It comes from coherence – aligning values with daily practice; pairing freedom with responsibility; designing environments that treat adolescence as a formative period worthy of care, structure, and trust. It comes from adults willing to hold authority with restraint, to accept limits, and to do the slow, often invisible work required to sustain culture over time. It carries a cost, or perhaps an investment, that matures gradually and compounds through consistency and attention.

This book does not argue that these schools represent the future of education, nor that their approaches can be easily transplanted elsewhere. They operate within real constraints of access, history, scale, and power, and they do not claim exemption from the tensions those constraints create. What distinguishes them is not escape from limitation, but the seriousness with which they choose within it.

If *Elevate* offers anything beyond the individual chapters it contains, it is not instruction or endorsement, but the illumination that emerges when these stories are read together. A clearer view of what it looks like when educational environments are designed with intention rather than inherited assumptions, default practices, or unexamined routines. A reminder that values shape experience only when they are lived. And an invitation to take responsibility – wherever one has it – for the spaces young people inhabit.

What *Elevate* ultimately makes visible is that coherence is neither accidental nor incidental, but actively chosen. It is enacted through how responsibility is shared, authority is exercised, structure is designed, and care is sustained – and it requires real labor, cost, and ongoing investment.

Such coherence is not designed for passive consumption, but for participation. These schools take responsibility for shaping who young people are becoming right now, and when adolescence is taken seriously as a period with its own moral weight, the present matters as much as what comes next. While metric-driven outcomes may follow, they are not the singular objective. Choosing to build or sustain this kind of learning community is a deliberate, labor-intensive ethical commitment – and choosing not to is an equally consequential decision that shapes young lives.

The recognition that sparked this project has not been resolved. It has been clarified, deepened, and given language. What readers do with that understanding, and how they carry it into their own contexts, questions, and choices, is left open.

Appendix A

Methodology and Advisory Board

This book grew out of conversation, not calculation. The schools included in *Elevate* were not selected through a formal research protocol, nor through a comprehensive or representative survey of boarding schools in the United States or abroad. Instead, they emerged through a nomination-based process shaped by professional experience, repeated exposure, and sustained dialogue with educators, clinicians, school leaders, and families who spend their lives thinking about adolescent development and educational environments.

How Schools Were Selected

Schools did not pay to be included in this project, nor were they compensated for their participation. Inclusion reflected nomination followed by interest, alignment with the project's intent, and the practical capacity to participate within the scope and timeframe of the work. The initial list of schools was assembled through an iterative process. We began by identifying schools that, in our own experience, seemed to be grappling intentionally with the question of holistic education – schools where academic rigor, residential life, community norms, and student responsibility appeared to be meaningfully integrated rather than siloed. From there, we solicited input from colleagues and advisors across education, mental health, and youth development, asking a simple question: *Which schools stand out to you as doing this work thoughtfully, and why?*

As names surfaced repeatedly, patterns began to emerge. Some schools were included because of long-standing reputations; others because of specific programs, structures, or cultural choices that reflected a deeper alignment between values and daily practice. The final list reflects both convergence and curiosity. It is intentionally incomplete, shaped by access, relationships, time, and the practical constraints of inviting schools to contribute substantial written reflections.

This process was, by design, unscientific. It privileges depth over breadth, coherence over comparison, and lived experience over formal proof. The resulting collection should be read as a snapshot – one moment in an ongoing and much larger conversation about education, adolescence, and community.

Advisory Perspectives

Throughout the development of this project, we benefited from the insight and perspective of an advisory group made up of educators, clinicians, school leaders, and practitioners whose work sits at the intersection of learning, mental health, and adolescent development. Their contributions took many forms: suggesting schools to consider, offering feedback on framing and language, challenging assumptions, and helping us see blind spots we might otherwise have missed.

This advisory group did not function as an editorial board, nor did its members review or approve individual school chapters. Responsibility for the final content of this book rests solely with the authors and the contributing schools, who were responsible only for their own discrete contribution. We are nonetheless deeply grateful for the time, thoughtfulness, and candor these advisors brought to the process, and we acknowledge the ways in which their thinking shaped the questions this book asks – even when their influence is not explicitly visible on the page.

Advisory Board

- Brad Bates – Head of School (through 2026), Dublin School (NH)
- John Kaufman – Head of School, Middlebridge School (RI)
- Meg Lahey – Educational Consultant, Steinbrecher Educational Advisors (CT)
- Holly Treat – Educational Consultant, The Bertram Group (CT)
- Sarah Wagner – School Psychologist, Epping School District (NH)
- Dr. Will White – Author (*Stories from the Field, A History of Wilderness Therapy*), Podcaster (Stories from the Field), Co-Founder, Summit Achievement (NH)
- Jenney Wilder – Founder, AllKindsOfTherapy.com (ME)
- Matthew Woodhall – Head of School, The Woodhall School (CT)

Intellectual Lineage and Influences

Elevate does not exist in isolation. It is informed by earlier efforts to surface educational environments that resist reduction to rankings, test scores, or narrow definitions of success. Two influences are particularly relevant. *Colleges That Change Lives* foregrounds the idea of educational fit over prestige, inviting readers to consider how alignment between student and institution matters more than status alone. *Stories from the Field* models a different but equally important commitment: allowing organizations to tell their own stories, in their own voices, without being flattened into a single interpretive frame.

This book shares elements of both impulses while taking a distinct approach. It does not attempt comparison, validation, or outcome analysis.

It does not argue that the schools included here are "better" than others (either included or omitted), nor does it seek to generalize their practices. Its contribution is narrower and more modest: to capture how a group of contemporary boarding schools understand and articulate their own work, in their own voices, at a particular moment in time.

Limits and Responsibilities

Transparency about process does not eliminate responsibility; it clarifies it. The choices reflected in this book – who is included, who is not, which voices are amplified – carry ethical weight. We acknowledge the paradox that any curated collection necessarily draws boundaries, including some while excluding others, and that those boundaries exist within broader systems of access, privilege, and opportunity.

Our hope is that by naming these limits openly, readers can engage the material with appropriate context and discernment. *Elevate* is not offered as a definitive account of holistic education, nor as an endorsement of any single model. It is offered as an honest attempt to listen closely, to notice patterns, and to contribute meaningfully to an ongoing conversation about how educational communities shape the lives of young people.

Appendix B

Questions for Reflection and Conversation

The questions that follow are not offered as a checklist, evaluation tool, or model for implementation. They are intended as prompts for reflection – ways of noticing alignment, tension, and choice within educational environments of many kinds.

They are written to be read from different positions of relationship to a community – by those who design and lead it, those who live and work within it, and those who choose engagement with it – without assuming a single or authoritative vantage point.

Some may resonate immediately; others may feel uncomfortable, irrelevant, or premature. That variation is expected. These questions are meant to be engaged slowly, selectively, and in conversation, rather than answered comprehensively or all at once.

Purpose and Coherence

- Where do the stated values of this environment show up clearly in daily life – and where do they quietly recede?
- Which aspects of the culture appear intentionally shaped, and which seem to persist largely by habit?
- What tends to be protected when pressures arise, and what is more easily compromised?

- How closely does the language used to describe young people align with how they actually experience the setting?

Structure and Daily Experience

- Which routines, schedules, or expectations appear to support growth and which primarily serve convenience or student management?
- Where does structure create clarity and safety, and where does it unintentionally limit agency?
- How visible and consistent is adult presence in the informal spaces where culture is reinforced or eroded?
- What parts of the day feel most meaningful or formative, and why?

Responsibility and Participation

- What responsibilities do young people hold that genuinely matter to the functioning of the community?
- Where are they invited into accountability, and where is responsibility quietly absorbed by adults?
- How are mistakes treated – as disruptions to be managed, or as moments for learning and repair?
- In what ways are young people positioned as contributors to the community rather than consumers of it?

Adult Roles and Authority

- How consistent are adult responses across roles, settings, and moments of stress?
- How is adult authority structured so that students experience

both meaningful relationships and safe ways to raise concerns?

- Where does culture depend heavily on individual adults, and where is it held collectively?
- How is authority exercised, and what balance exists between clarity, relationship, and positional power?
- What support do adults receive to sustain presence, alignment, and care over time?

Limits, Tradeoffs, and Choice

- What constraints – financial, cultural, historical – most shape what is possible in this context?
- Where does the environment demonstrate restraint in service of coherence, and where has expansion come at a cost?
- How is the tension managed between individual student wellbeing and the protection of adults, the community, or organizational reputation??
- What does saying "no" look like here, and who bears the weight of that decision?
- Which young people tend to thrive in this setting, and which may struggle, even when support is present?

Time, Development, & Differences

- How does the pace of this environment support, or undermine, healthy development?
- Where is there pressure to demonstrate progress quickly, and how is that pressure handled?
- What forms of growth are hardest to notice or measure here?
- How is the distinction made between short-term performance and longer-term development?

- Where is the approach to pluralism most successful and most tested, and how is the tension between *fair* and *equal* navigated?
- How does the community speak about learning differences or mental health challenges, and what is clearly within – and beyond – its capacity to support?

Closing Questions

- If this environment were being designed today, what might be chosen intentionally and what might be reconsidered?
- What aspects of the community feel most alive, and what feels performative or brittle?
- Where does coherence feel strongest, and where does it seem most fragile?
- Given the influence adults have on young people's daily lives, what responsibilities does that influence create now?

Acknowledgements

This book exists because a group of schools agreed to participate with openness, trust, and generosity. We are deeply grateful to each of the schools included in *Elevate* – not simply for their willingness to be represented, but for their willingness to speak in their own voices, on their own terms. Writing honestly about one's values, structures, and daily practices requires care and vulnerability. We respect the effort each school made to do so, and the trust they placed in us by sharing their perspectives with integrity and candor.

We are also grateful to the educators, clinicians, consultants, and practitioners who served as advisors throughout the life of this project. Their perspectives helped shape the questions we asked, the schools we considered, and the assumptions we worked to examine. Responsibility for the synthesis, framing, and final content of this book rests with the authors, while contributing schools retain responsibility for their individual chapters. The thinking of many others nevertheless sharpened the work and improved its clarity, and we appreciate that guidance deeply.

Several individuals offered particular generosity at key moments – by reading drafts, challenging language, naming blind spots, providing encouragement or introductions, or by asking better questions than we were asking ourselves. Their engagement strengthened the work in ways that may not always be visible on the page, but were essential to its development. Special thanks to Holly Treat, Sarah Wagner, Will White, and

Jenney Wilder for their active, at times continuous and at times pivotal, participation in this project.

This work also reflects both author's experiences and perspectives gathered over decades of exposure to, and participation in, holistic educational communities. Jake extends special thanks to the broader Mansfield Hall community, and especially to Jasmine Lamb, whose belief in the power of holistic education and the formative potential of community has influenced much of the thinking that made this book possible.

We are grateful to our partners, families, and colleagues for their patience and support throughout this process. Writing a book is rarely a solitary endeavor, even when much of the work happens alone. We appreciate the space that was made for this project, and the steady encouragement that allowed it to continue.

Finally, we thank the readers of *Elevate*. This book was written in the hope that it would be read thoughtfully and without haste. If it prompts careful conversation, reflection, or renewed attentiveness to how educational environments shape the lived experiences of young people, then it has served its purpose.

About the Authors

Jake Weld

Born in upstate New York and raised in North Carolina, Jake has worked in a wide range of educational settings across the United States. His early experiences in summer camp and outdoor experiential programs shaped a long-standing interest in community, adolescence and young adulthood, and intentional approaches to whole-person development. He has served as a classroom teacher, Dean of Academics, Assistant Head, and Head of School at boarding schools in California, North Carolina, and Vermont.

Jake holds a Master's degree in Education, a high school social studies teaching credential, and a B.S. in History. He currently serves as Chief Strategy Officer for Mansfield Hall and Canopy College Coaching, where he works alongside educational communities as they examine how their structures, cultures, and practices shape students' experiences during periods of transition. He is also the founder of Considered Practice, an independent platform exploring the intersection of structure, culture, innovation, and education. Jake lives in Vermont with his partner, Molly.

Jeremy McGeorge

Originally from Michigan, Jeremy began his career working in outdoor and experiential education, providing direct student care within the outdoor behavioral health field. He has since served in a range of roles across education, school leadership, and behavioral health care, including program development, school administration, and national-level hospital administration. His work has taken him to therapeutic programs and boarding schools in the Berkshires, northern Vermont, Utah, Arizona, Costa Rica, and beyond.

Jeremy holds a B.A. in Psychology from the University of Arizona and a B.S. in Biology from Northern Arizona University. He lives in Western Massachusetts with his wife, Laura, a boarding school nurse, and their two children. Jeremy is a partner at The Bertram Group, an educational consulting firm working across school, college, and graduate placements, including therapeutic and behavioral healthcare settings.

Their Partnership

Longtime colleagues and friends, Jake and Jeremy have spent more than five decades collectively working in and around educational communities, including boarding schools. Both continue to visit schools regularly as part of their professional work.

This project grew out of a shared recognition, formed over years of practice and observation, that some schools are doing something quietly but meaningfully different in how they approach adolescence, community, and education. *Elevate* reflects their effort to capture, contextualize, and amplify these stories, and to begin understanding what they reveal when considered together, while preserving the voices of the schools themselves.

www.ingramcontent.com/pod-product-compliance
Lightning Source LLC
LaVergne TN
LVHW100519110826
845146LV00002B/702
9798994964200